CHANGE YOUR BRAIN CHANGE YOUR LIFE!

CHANGE YOUR BRAIN CHANGE YOUR LIFE!

SONDRA KORNBLATT

JAICO PUBLISHING HOUSE

Ahmedabad Bangalore Chennai
Delhi Hyderabad Kolkata Mumbai

Published by Jaico Publishing House
A-2 Jash Chambers, 7-A Sir Phirozshah Mehta Road
Fort, Mumbai - 400 001
jaicopub@jaicobooks.com
www.jaicobooks.com

Published in arrangement with
Red Wheel/Weiser, LLC
65, Parker Street, Suite 7
Newburyport, MA 01950, USA

To be sold only in India, Bangladesh, Bhutan,
Pakistan, Nepal, Sri Lanka and the Maldives.

CHANGE YOUR BRAIN, CHANGE YOUR LIFE!
ISBN 978-93-86867-12-4

First Jaico Impression: 2017
Seventh Jaico Impression: 2025

Printed by
Trinity Academy For Corporate Training Limited, Mumbai

With love to my husband Howard, who died before seeing this book published. His active brain, loving heart, fatherly care, and deep spirit brought joy to our two decades together.

Contents

Foreword

Annaliese, a forty-two-year-old office manager, made an appointment to see me about Alzheimer's disease. She was sure she had it because she constantly misplaced her purse, forgot meetings, and couldn't remember names when she ran into old friends. While the memory results of her mental status exam didn't indicate serious cognitive loss, we spent some time talking about how Annaliese's brain could work better. I suggested she improve her sleep habits, be mindful of her diet, add some fish oil and other supplements, and examine how stress is created in her life.

The next time Annaliese visits, I will show her *Change Your Brain, Change Your Life!* and she can peruse the hundreds of great ideas it contains—tried-and-true ideas and innovative complementary methods for enhancing the function of the brain.

During more than twenty-six years practicing medicine, I have seen results of practice using treatments that I learned in conventional medicines as well as those I have learned from more alternative practitioners and literature. I know what is sound. In this book, Sondra Kornblatt has created a balanced and holistic view of a healthy brain. All the methods in this book, conventional or alternative, are well researched and easy to understand. She addresses brain development from exercise and energy medicine to memory and meditation. Some of her suggestions are clever reminders for common brain-boosting ideas: exercise, eating vegetables, and getting fish oil. In other areas, she blends nutrition, aromatherapy, energy medicine, and more to compile intriguing ideas for the brain:

- Cinnamon—even a whiff of it—improves learning.
- Body alignment (balanced posture) increases brain blood flow.
- Rooms painted with contrasting colors stimulate learning.
- Volunteering reduces depression and stimulates the same pleasure center for eating and sex.
- Laughter Yoga classes or laughter tapes release healing laughter.
- Swinging arms when you walk works the two hemispheres of your brain.
- Fear can be reduced with psychological acupressure such as Tapas Acupressure Techniques (TAT).
- Creativity can be enhanced by nodding your head.

That's just a start. *Change Your Brain* also provides a comprehensive list of toxins to avoid (from treated wood to new shower curtains) and good foods to eat (from saffron to avocado). This book covers the whole range of brain health with humor and respect for the amazing human body.

Studies have shown that attitude is critical in healthy brain function. *Change Your Brain, Change Your Life!* will help you support the attitude that respects your brain.

—Fernando Vega, M.D., Seattle, Washington

Acknowledgments

It took a village to raise a brain book: my wonderful community sustained me and my brain during the writing process. Let me introduce them to you.

The generous and helpful people I interviewed taught me so much more than would fit in this book. Deepest appreciation to Ragini Michaels, Dr. Fernando Vega, Dr. Joan Borysenko, Sally Kempton (Swami Durgananda), Narayana Granatelli, Dr. Eric Chudler, David Stizhal, Dr. Todd Clements, Dr. James Dalgren, Christopher Mascis, Dr. Ralph Kenney, Sharon Begley, Dr. Eric Maisel, Renna Shesso, and Carrie Lafferty.

My writing community provided sage editorial and expert advice, along with large doses of encouragement, particularly when I struggled with summarizing *emotions* in 250 words. Much gratitude to Anne Kornblatt, Ann Gonzalez, Jodi Forschmiedt (especially for help editing the final manuscript), Priscilla Long, Dr. Jean Milican, Sharon Maffett, Auky Van Beek, David Stitzhal, editors Caroline Pincus, Pam Suwinsky, and Brenda Knight, and the Seattle public libraries.

My friends and family buoyed me on the journey. Much love to Diane Rodriguez, whose support remains after she's gone. Michael Pitrone, Sonja Carson, and the Soiree community helped me laugh at myself and my stories. My parents gave support and love on many levels. Love to Howard, Milo, and Ella, who got sick of hearing about omega-3s and celebrated completed chapters at the dining room table.

You've all made my brain so much stronger—not to mention my heart. *Merci.*

Note: Although I used the names of family, friends, and clients in the book, the examples in the book are composites. Even you, Mom. I've tried to accurately represent what my sources have told me, but I take responsibility for any misinterpretations or inaccuracies. This book does not include footnotes because they are so distracting. However, in the Bibliography and Resources section at the back of the book, I've listed the sources that I've used in my research.

Introduction

Change Your Brain, Change Your Life

Change is inevitable—except from a vending machine.

—Robert C. Gallagher

Can't remember the name of your doctor when you see him at the store? Forget your standing appointment for physical therapy? Worried about Alzheimer's?

Chances are, you're not stupid, rude, nor experiencing early dementia. Instead, your brain is frazzled: unhealthy habits, aging, long work hours, and information overload. Even with all this stress, you're *not* at a brain-dead end.

That's because your brain is changing. It changes every day, even as you read this sentence. "The principal activities of brains are making changes in themselves," says Dr. Marvin Minsky in his book *Society of the Mind.*

You can support your brain by . . . changing it more. When you create new connections, your brain becomes stronger. Your neurons (brain cells) get active and your brain stays plastic, able to create new neural pathways.

How do we know this? From new technology and research. In the past decade, technology such as SPECT (single photon emission computed tomography) scans and functional MRIs (magnetic resonance imagings) have shown brainwaves and brain function in action. Scientists have learned that the brain generates new neurons throughout life, that meditation increases gamma waves, and that movement changes thoughts.

Just reading about brain research is enough to make your neurons fire.

Researchers have also learned that stimulation keeps your brain engaged and growing. Stimulation isn't a loud disco arcade of flashing lights. It means doing something different to deepen and create new brain pathways. Otherwise known as making changes.

You can make huge changes (go back for your degree in speech pathology) or smaller ones (notice your feet in your shoes). Change what you eat, how you move, your environment, memory, learning, creativity, and emotions. They all stretch the brain and keep it active.

You'll find hundreds of boosters to transform the brain in the chapters of this book, such as:

- Using your nondominant hand (the left for most of us) to brush your teeth
- Avoiding toxins in smelly plastics
- Cross-crawling (touching your right hand to your left knee and vice versa several times) to link your hemispheres

- Tapping points on your body to help emotions release
- Eating foods that make you smarter
- Imagining giant wacky images to remember your grocery list

Most of these changes are easy to make. However, habits, comforts, and identity may get in the way. You could feel odd or self-conscious when you try something new. You may want to quit before the change becomes a habit. That's just your neurons not knowing each other—yet. Give them a little time.

Here's some help to make brain changes:

- Don't do all the boosters in the book. First off, you don't have time. Second, practicing one or two boosters helps deepen your knowledge and ability—a key brain stretcher.
- Explore boosters that intrigue you. They'll feel right, toot your horn, send off fireworks. Stretch, but find a stretch you'll enjoy.
- Feel free to focus on just one chapter, or pick a booster from a few different ones. While it might be hard to practice three memory stretchers, you might enjoy adding a veggie, playing a word game, and drawing for five minutes at lunch.
- To create a habit, make a note each time you practice the booster. Put a sticker on your calendar, write

about it in your blog, or form a "Brain Support" group to crow with. After twenty-one days, the wisdom goes, it will become more routine.

- When that new booster becomes old hat . . . it's time to stretch your brain again. Find another one to engage those little neurons. Keep this book in a convenient place—the bedroom, bathroom, or the car. Then it's easy to find new ways to stretch your brain, even when you wait for your children to get out of school.

From boosters to information, this book helps the brain—it changed mine. During months of research, I studied how the emotions, meditation, memory, body-mind environment, creativity, movement, and thinking all interact. I talked to many wise scholars and authors, developing an appreciation for the amazing organ under the skull.

Before I added brain-stretchers to the book, I tried them out. While I didn't become a member of Mensa, I found I could shake up my neurons so they connected better. My family will attest to my changes:

- I've become a fish oil fanatic. In fact, my kids cover their ears and say *na-na-na-na-na* when I talk about the power of omega-3s—again!

- I leave the store when I notice an uncomfortable smell. In one case, it was the out-gassing of new carpet, which is bad for the brain.

- I pace the room to recharge my thoughts and calm stress.
- I appreciate stillness in meditation, to balance the constant movement of thoughts.

As you change your brain, you'll also change your life, by becoming more connected to your senses and feeling more alive. Your awareness will grow, you'll be able to make better, more informed choices, and even appreciate the beauty you may have forgotten.

What do you change? Focus on three areas:

Body, with smart food, movement, healthy environment, and rest

Emotional response, which changes your perspective on life

Thoughts and beliefs, through imagining new possibilities.

You'll engage the whole function of the brain, to tap into life.

So take your brain for a ride, let it see the sights. You'll appreciate the miracle that lives under the skull. And the gift of being alive.

1

A Short Tour of the Brain

The brain has the storage capacity of 6 million years of the Wall Street Journal.

—Greg Iles, *Footprints of God*

You are the proud owner of the most complex organ in the entire world: your brain. In fact, if the brain weren't so complicated, we couldn't begin to understand it. There are more connections in your brain than there are stars in the universe.

Those connections are all coordinated with each other. So when you hit a rock while riding your bike, your brain notices and acts instantaneously. *Uh-oh, balance is askew, veer the torso in the opposite direction while the foot swings to the ground.* The brain saved your skull, even if you scratched your leg. Meanwhile it generates memories and words so you can tell your coworkers the story.

> There are more connections in your brain than there are stars in the universe.

For millennia, people have wondered how the brain works. Scientists autopsied cadavers, analyzed brain injuries, and monitored reactions to brain surgery. They located specific areas—for instance, Broca's area processes speech—but it took until the 1990s to reveal how the whole brain interacted.

Cutting-edge technology—such as functional MRIs (magnetic resonance imagings) and SPECT (single photon emission computed tomography) scans—revealed the brain in action: How exercise and meditation changed brainwaves. How creativity doesn't live just in the right hemisphere. How idle brain areas take on new uses after injury.

Keeping up with the new information is a brain booster. However, if you're pressed for time, here's a short and simple tour of the brain. (To delve deeper into how the brain works, check out *A User's Guide to the Brain* by John Ratey or Neuroscience for Kids at the University of Washington, at *http://faculty.washington.edu/chudler/index1.html.*)

The Giant Walnut

You have a giant walnut under your skull—only it's pinkish-gray and soft, like custard. It's suspended in membranes and crystal-clear fluid within the hard shell of your skull.

The brain evolved from that of reptiles to mammals to humans, creating three main layers (illustrated in Figure 1.1) that surround and interact with each other.

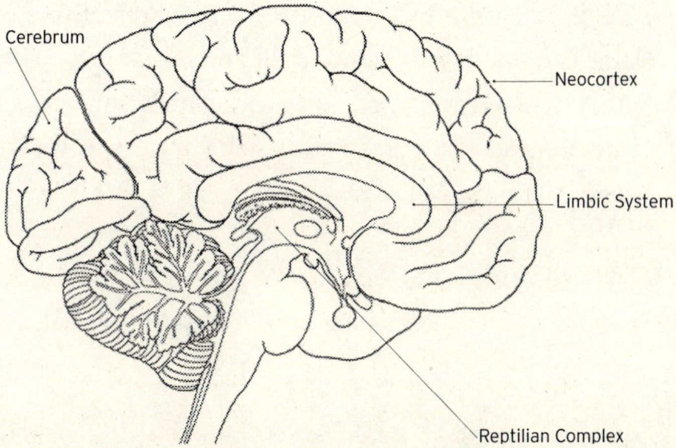

Figure 1.1 The three layers of the brain

- The primitive or reptile brain (reptilian complex) is the first level, at the bottom. It includes the brain stem and the cerebellum, a strawberry-shaped clump of cells just below the cerebrum. This part controls sleep, waking, breathing, temperature, and basic automatic movements (such as heartbeat, balance, even bike riding). It also acts as a way station for sensory input—it helps evaluate safety and determine the need for quick response.
- The mammalian or limbic brain (limbic system) is the second level. It develops memory and emotions for social interactions through the hippocampus, which looks like two seahorses, one on each side of the brain. Severe damage to the hippocampus can cause amnesia. The limbic system also coordinates movements and promotes group survival.
- The third level is the neocortex, including the two large cerebral hemispheres, right and left. It fine-tunes the lower functions, creates abstract thinking, consciousness, and creativity. It's able to plan as well as react to new challenges.

The neocortex is the top layer, or gray matter, of the brain. It evolved most recently and is only found in mammals.

The Anatomy of the Brain

Within these three levels are specialized structures that work in concert.

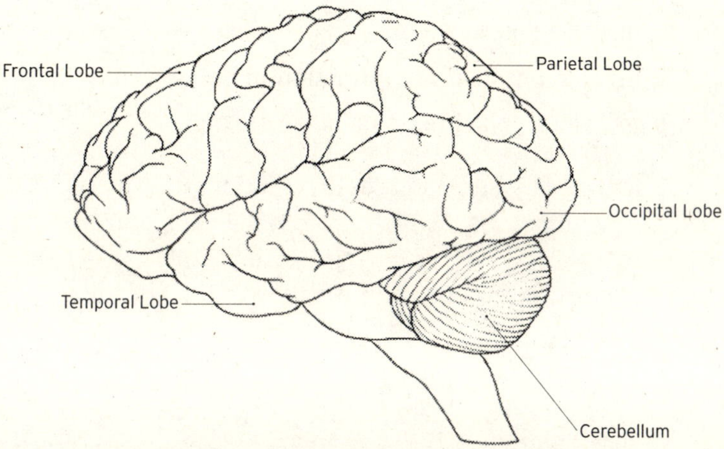

Figure 1.2 The anatomy of the brain

- The **cerebellum** at the base of the brain keeps the action, emotions, language, and memories in tune.
- The cerebrum divides its function into four **lobes,** illustrated in Figure 1.2. The **occipital lobe** is the visual processing center. The **parietal lobe** coordinates sensory and special information to make sense of the world around you and to monitor how you relate physically to others. It interacts with language, math, body image and function, and drawing. The

frontal lobe behind the forehead has intricate connections to other areas in the brain. It regulates emotions, thought, sense of self, verbal activity, and problem solving, to name a few. It produces and evaluates speech, expressions, empathy and genuineness. The **temporal lobe** is the auditory processing center; it makes meaning of speech and vision and is involved in memory formation. It contains the *hippocampus,* the brain's memory indexer.

- The **limbic** system focuses on emotions and social bonds.
- The **cingulate gyrus** in the midbrain directs our response to others.

Brain Components

Why is your brain shaped like a walnut? To maximize the thinking area. The cerebrum (the largest part of the brain) and the cerebellum (which coordinates movement and lies below the cerebrum) are coated with gray matter called the corte (Latin, meaning "bark"). The **cerebral cortex** (the outer layer of the cerebrum) is where most of the information processing (thinking) takes place. The cerebral cortex is huge. If you stretched it out flat it would be the size of several sheets of newspaper. Folded and wrinkled, it fits those clever neurons under your skull. The folds in the cerebral cortex increase the available surface area and gray matter, so that more information can be processed.

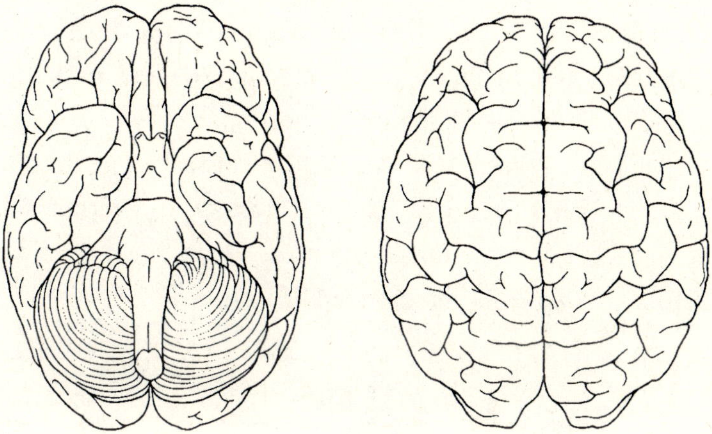

Figure 1.3 The two cerebral hemispheres

The cerebrum has two hemispheres (see Figure 1.3), each with some specialized functions. The left hemisphere is more analytical, specializing in language, math, and logic. The right hemisphere specializes in spatial abilities, music, visual imagery, and recognition. However, the hemispheres interact much more than was once thought. The pathway between them is the *corpus callosum,* a band of 200-250 million nerve fibers.

Brain Cells

Good connections make the brain work well. Connections are made by neurons (nerve or brain cells), which transmit information through an electrochemical process. Neurons are shaped like a sapling tree: a branch of dendrites at one end receives information and an axon at the other end sends information. (See Figure 1.4.) The brain contains more than a hundred billion neurons, each with one axon and as many as 100,000 dendrites (communication transmitters and receivers). Electrical impulses release chemicals called neurotransmitters, which trigger or inhibit actions, and determine the strength of your emotional responses. Neurotransmitters flow across a synapse—a gap between neurons.

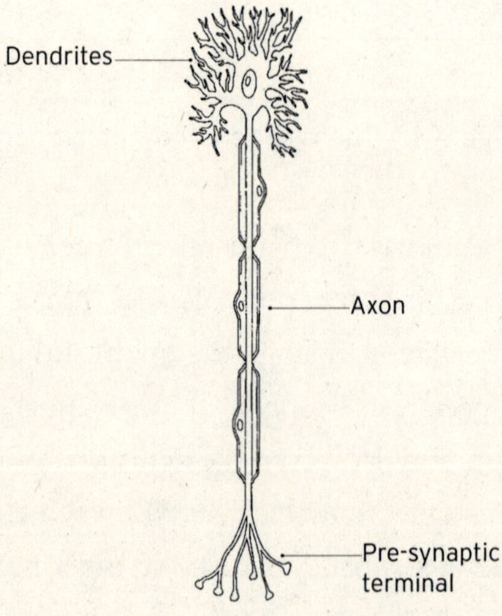

Figure 1.4 Illustration of neuron, showing axon and dendrites

A series of individual connections create a route through your brain called a neuropathway. The more you practice something, the more you deepen neuropathways as you strengthen skills, habits, and memories—which could apply to a Bach minuet or nail-biting. When you learn something new, or when you make a change, you create new pathways. Your brain becomes more flexible and resilient.

Mirror neurons fire when you see someone performing an action—including the action of having a feeling. These mirror neurons make emotions contagious, according to Daniel Goleman in *Social Intelligence*, so even non-baseball fans get excited when their city's team goes to the World Series.

Brain Activity and Brain Waves

As your brain moves through different activities, from concentrating to sleeping, it produces electrical fluctuations. Scientists have measured those rhythmic electrical fluctuations of the brain with electroencephalogram (EEG) and correlated them to various activities. The cycles per second are labeled with Greek letters, such as beta (active and busy) to alpha (relaxing) to gamma (meditating monks).

Neurogenesis

Until the 1990s, scientists thought your brain stopped generating new neurons as an adult. If a brain cell gave its life, these scientists said, there were no replacement parts. Now we know that at age seventy-five, you still have all the neuron connections you did at twenty-five, though lack of mental exercise may make those connections slower. Your brain continues to grow new neurons (in a process called *neurogenesis*), 500 to 1,000 each day.

> At age seventy-five, you still have all the neuron connections you did at twenty-five.

The brain also includes trillions of *glia*, or supportive cells. They feed, guide, coat, and support neurons. The brain also has many vascular cells for its large blood supply that keep the neurons pumped with oxygen and glucose.

Most of these components have been know for centuries or decades. What's new is understanding how these components function.

The Working Brain

Back in the old days (when Ronald Reagan was president) scientists imagined the brain as a series of containers—like a silverware divider. Each task had its own little slot. Thinking stayed separate from feeling, memory, language, and movement.

In the 1990s, scientists used functional MRIs to detect changes in activity in the brain. Researchers discovered that the brain is more like an ecosystem than a stagnant silverware divider. All the parts interact with each other.

In fact, the brain is a self-operating system, says Dr. Nancy Andreasen in her book, *The Creating Brain.* A self-operating system operates like a flock of starlings: the whole group instantaneously veers to one side, then the other, without stopping for a meeting to decide what to do.

That's just what your brain does when you're falling off your bike.

Through a rapid-fire series of connections, the structures of your brain talk to each other and produce an instantaneous response that is intelligent, even though you don't have to think about it. Thanks to your brain, you can walk away from the accident with your skull intact.

How to Protect Your Brain

Movement can help or hurt the brain. Consider how delicate the brain is, crammed into the hard skull. An injury can occur even without the loss of consciousness.

Dr. Daniel Amen recommends some boosters for protecting it:

- Think about your brain before you do activities that might put it at risk—even for a mild concussion.
- Wear protective gear while playing sports (especially important for kids). Don't hit a soccer ball with your head.
- Fasten your seatbelt. Avoid motorcycles.
- Wear a helmet when you ride a bike.
- Walk facing automobile traffic, so you and the driver can see each other.
- Use ladders to reach something high—not chairs or countertops.
- Protect the brains of babies and toddlers: don't shake these small children. Use appropriate car seats.
- Protect young children from falling down stairs.

Respecting and understanding your brain pays homage to the amazing organ it is. So the two of you can keep each other around for a long time.

2

Not All in Your Head

The Body-Mind

Lost in thought. (Please send rescue party.)

—SLOGAN ON A T-SHIRT

Barbara was on a mad quest for her keys. She hunted in her pocketbook, on the counter, in her coat pockets, beneath the car seat, and in the front door. "I had them when I came in . . . or was the door unlocked?" She checked her pocketbook again.

Her mind was racing. She imagined random places she had been as she came into the house. She chastised herself for being disorganized and late to her meeting. Then back to the lost keys. Barbara was disconnected from her body and couldn't focus.

"I've lost my mind."

But maybe she was so caught in her mind, she couldn't access the wisdom of her body.

What is the mind? Is it your thoughts, brain, unconscious beliefs? We usually don't think about the mind; we just take it for granted. We have to, in order to get anything done.

Still, it's worth looking at the mind, whatever you consider it to be. When you understand the mind, you navigate it better, learn more, and strengthen the brain through your increased consciousness.

We consider the 'mind' a *thing*—but it's not. Instead, the mind is a verb, says Dr. Karl Pribam, neuropsychology professor at Stanford Medical School. The mind is a process of mental activities: feeling, planning, remembering. And the process goes beyond the brain. The mind uses the body to function.

In fact, you have a "second brain" in your gut, with more nerve endings than you have under your skull.

The mind influences the body (you think you screwed up at work and you get a headache). The body influences the mind (a yoga class calms worried thoughts).

Here's proof of the body-mind connection: Imagine reading erotica about a hot, deep kiss. Whether it's romantic novels or porn, thoughts and images about sexuality clearly cause the body to respond.

The body also responds to thoughts about improving healing, athletic ability, and attitudes toward life. Images and attitude can lessen diseases such as irritable bowel syndrome, protect against heart disease, and help with the side effects of chemotherapy.

This chapter looks at the mind, the body, and how they work together.

The Mind of the Body-Mind

You can't see the mind. But people have been dissecting it for years, in philosophy, religion, and psychology. They've discovered and labeled

- Conscious mind
- Unconscious mind
- Ego

- Personality or id
- Identity
- Intellect
- Self-critic
- Inner child
- Drama queen
- Creative muse

You could also notice and label the time-twit or do-gooder in your own mind.

These concepts help you make sense of the mind. In turn, the mind makes sense of the world by creating . . . concepts. Otherwise known as stories.

Stories keep stimulation from overwhelming you—or they give meaning to it. When you're waiting for a bus and searching for your bus pass, you might not see the red lights. But when you're crossing the street, those red lights are guides to your personal safety.

Stories can be true objectively or can feel true subjectively. Both forms involve physical sensations. Ever get rapid heartbeat and increased perspiration when you're *sure* your boss won't like your proposal? That story makes your adrenaline pump. The reality makes you smile when your boss approves the idea.

Problems arise when emotions and thoughts limit the mind. Limits can be "anxiety, negative fantasies, pessimism, and even identity with certain ideas of who we and others are," says Dr. Joan Borysenko, former director of Harvard's Mind-Body Clinic and author of *Minding the Body, Mending the Mind.*

However, you can change your mind. You can create new synaptic pathways in the brain, helping its long term health. Key to changing your mind—and brain—can be focused on these three areas:

1. Alter your **emotional response,** which transforms the feeling of truth about a story.
2. Shift your **thoughts and beliefs,** substituting new images for fears and limits.
3. Change your **body** through exercise, sleep, and even laughter.

☆ Boosters: Change Your Mind ☆

These boosters engage the mind's perspective. Some attend to changing thoughts. Others work with emotions and the unconscious mind. Many are addressed in more depth in chapters 3, 4, and 8.

Cognitive Behavioral Therapy

Cognitive behavioral therapy (CBT) experts say that thoughts trigger emotions and behavior, though others debate whether thoughts automatically come first. However, CBT tools can alter automatic negative thoughts (often called ANTs), give new perspectives, and release mental tension. It may take a few months of practice to alleviate an "irrational thought process," say CBT practitioners.

- Track and change your thoughts by **keeping a diary.** Note events that trigger uncomfortable feelings, thoughts, and behaviors.

- **Reframe** incidents to provide a new perspective. Reframing is a natural process you move through as external circumstances and inner stories change. For example, if you have a small itch on your head, no big deal. But if your daughter's friend has head lice, each small itch becomes a fear of finding pests imbedded in your fingernails. Reframing can also be a conscious choice, giving more options in life. If you worry that your house is messy, reframe from seeing yourself as a slob to someone who cares; you spent time to read to your daughter instead of cleaning.

- **Snap a rubber band** on your wrist when you notice a thought pattern you want to change. Then remind yourself to substitute a more comforting thought.

Self-Talk

Have a dialogue with yourself. Talk back if you find yourself sunk in a negative story. Create a positive to balance the negative rather than trying to defeat it.

- Remind yourself that you are great, **everyone has personality quirks,** and you are loveable.

- Talk to your **inner child** or fearful self. Remind it that you are capable and can get help from others.

Address judgments and blame. Blame is a spiral of thoughts that perpetuates ongoing anger and frustration. Since you can't change others, focus on changing your own point of view. Ask yourself questions to determine if blame is a distracting story of your mind. These questions, based on the work of Byron Katie, are detailed in chapter 4.

Practices

Notice what you let into your mind. Buddhist meditation teacher Sally Kempton says that when we dwell on a lot of negative thoughts, we tell "ourselves stories about everything that's wrong with us and the world." It's not fun to live in that kind of world. Change the hold negative ideas have on your mind. Replace them with their opposites. For instance, if your father-in-law drives you crazy with nit-picking, remember that he is kind to his grandkids.

- Another method is to spend 20 minutes repeating positive thoughts, in a technique called **Metta** or **Loving-Kindness Meditation** in Buddhist practice. You wish peace for yourself and those around you, even people in the news with whom you get upset.

- **Short-Term Dynamic Therapy** is intensive psychotherapy that addresses blocked emotions and limiting beliefs. Techniques focus and intensify traditional psychotherapy, achieving structural changes in briefer time periods.

- Change the inner logic of the mind using **neuro-linguistic programming** (NLP). NLP is an interpersonal communications model and an alternative approach to psychotherapy, based on modeling the exceptional behavior and communication abilities of three successful psychotherapists. NLP techniques use reframing, visualization, and body-mind strategies to change ingrained patterns of emotions, behavior, and responses.

- **Meditation** creates space around thoughts—no coincidence that it's called *mindfulness*. (See chapter 7 for more on meditation techniques.)

The Body of the Body-Mind

To get another perspective on the mind, let's look at the mind through the body's perspective. Have you heard of phantom limb syndrome? That's when someone still feels itching, pain, and sensations of a limb that's been lost.

Turns out, it's not just the desire for the missing arm or leg. When the brain no longer receives the sensory input from the missing limb, it reprograms the underused area. It's a slow process, but even a few neurons make a big difference, according to Vanderbilt University. A Vanderbilt doctor did sensory tests on a blindfolded patient who had lost his arm. When the doctor dribbled water down the left cheek, the patient swore his missing arm got wet.

The changing brain had responded to the body by reorganizing idle neurons.

You can use your body to change your thoughts, emotions, and beliefs as well as by expanding the connections in the brain. These boosters show you how.

☆ Boosters: Humor and Laughter ☆

The response to humor—especially laughter—releases stress, aids immunity, changes moods for the better, helps you think, and improves memory.

Found on T-shirts:

> Instant human—Just add coffee.
>
> Protons have mass? I didn't even know they were Catholic.
>
> They say I have ADD but they just don't underst . . .
> Oh look! A chicken!

If you chuckled, that's good for your brain.

Laughter releases stress, aids immunity, changes moods for the better, helps you think, and improves memory.

The new field of *gelotology* is exploring the benefits of laughter. It was brought to public awareness in Norman Cousins's memoir *Anatomy of an Illness.* Cousins found that comedies, like those of the Marx Brothers, helped him feel better and get some pain-free sleep. That's because laughter helps the pituitary gland release its own pain-suppressing opiates.

More on Laughter

Laughter also:

- Lowers blood pressure
- Increases vascular blood flow and oxygenation of the blood
- Gives a workout to the diaphragm and abdominal, respiratory, facial, leg, and back muscles
- Reduces certain stress hormones such as cortisol and adrenaline

- Increases the response of tumor- and disease-killing cells such as Gamma-interferon and T-cells
- Defends against respiratory infections—even reducing the frequency of colds—by increasing immunoglobulin in saliva
- Increases memory and learning; in a study at Johns Hopkins University Medical School, humor during instruction led to increased test scores
- Improves alertness, creativity, and memory

Humor and creativity work in similar ways, says humor guru William Fry, M.D., of Stanford University, by creating relationships between two disconnected items, engaging the whole brain.

Humor works quickly. Less than a half-second after exposure to something funny, an electrical wave moves through the higher brain functions of the cerebral cortex. The left hemisphere analyzes the words and structure of the joke; the right hemisphere "gets" the joke; the visual sensory area of the occipital lobe creates images; the limbic (emotional) system makes you happier; and the motor sections make you smile or laugh.

Increase your brain workout with some giggles:

- **Find out what's funny.** Something's funny when you snort milk out of your nose—but what makes you laugh? Absurd humor replaces the familiar with the unexpected. Wile E. Coyote chases Road Runner after being smashed by a piano. Superior humor—like lawyer and blonde jokes—rearrange life's hierarchies. In dark humor, you laugh at what scares you.

- **Laugh without a joke.** Laughter may also be about relationships, says Robert Provine, professor at the University of Maryland. In fact, you may be "tuned" for laughter from family and culture. It helps you cope with life—or a rude in-law—by relieving mental and physical tensions.

- **Immerse yourself in humor.** Check out comedy books, movies, and tapes at the library or stores.

- **Trigger laughter.** Our mirror neurons trigger humor by hearing others laugh. Just like yawning, but more fun. *Ha.* Start smiling when you listen to this Web site of different recorded laughs: *http://www.psy.vanderbilt.edu/faculty/bachorowski/laugh.htm. Ha ha.* Or buy a laughter CD—60 minutes of chuckles. *Ha ha ha.* Great background noise for a party.

- **Read the comics** in your newspaper or online. From the traditional to the odd—*Baby Blues, Betty,* or *Bizarro,* they're a daily dose of humor.

- **Try laughter meditation,** consisting of stretching, laughing, and silence. It can transform your energy and mood.

- **Join a laughter club** or a Laughter Yoga class. Participants playfully imitate breathing and sounds of laughter, until simulated laughter turns into the real thing. They receive healing, company, humor, and the physical sensation of deep laughs.

☆ Boosters: Energy Medicine ☆

Energy is in breath, cells, and even chemicals of emotions and thoughts. Can touch or intention change your energy (and your emotions and thoughts)? Energy techniques, both centuries old and newly developed, say "Yes."

According to acupuncture, *qi gong* (methods focusing on the body's life force), and other ancient techniques, energy flows in "rivers" of energy called *meridians.* Some call this force of energy your *biofield.* Energy practitioners say changing this energy allows you to learn, relax, and heal—all good for your brain.

Although recent studies have shown the positive affect of acupuncture on health, there haven't been effective scientific measurements of energy fields. However, many people, including your author, have vouched for the effectiveness of energy techniques. See if these ways of changing energy in the body will work for you.

- **The crown pull** clears your head and mind, says Donna Eden in *Energy Medicine*. It also tingles the skull surrounding the brain. Put your thumbs at your temples and your fingertips on the bridge of your nose. Slowly, and with some pressure, pull your fingers apart to your thumbs—a little brow massage. Place your fingers in the middle of your forehead and pull to your thumbs. Repeat this pull by moving your fingers up your scalp all the way to the back of your head. Stretch your fingers out as you pull over your hair.

- **Yank on your ears.** It stimulates meridians that connect to the rest of your body. It can also loosen the interplay of bones surrounding your brain, according to craniosacral therapists. Gently tug all around the ears and the lobes, pulling along the natural lines of the ear. (For example, pull up at the top, back at the sides, and down at the lobes.) Hold the cartilage closer to the center, rather than the edges, if you feel pinched. You can do this very softly and still have good results.

- **Scratch your scalp** to bring blood flow to the brain. Lightly scratch the base of your head just above where the spine ends. Move to the side of your head and scratch your fingertips in an arc back and forth just outside your ears. The tingle lasts a few minutes after you're done.

- **Visit an energy medicine practitioner.** Energy therapies include acupuncture and acupressure (needles or pressure to relieve pain and treat conditions), BodyTalk (hands-on healing through helping body parts communicate), *qi gong* (body life force system), energy psychology (stimulating points on the skin to shift emotions), Reiki (transmit healing energy through the hands), Therapeutic Touch (nonsectarian laying-on of hands), Applied Kinesiology (muscle-strength testing to diagnose and determine treatment), medical intuitives (using intuition to find the cause of a physical or emotional condition), and intercessory prayer (prayer as a medium of healing). Get recommendations from friends or doctors, or find a teacher in the field. Trust your intuition as well, to determine if the practitioner or type of therapy is a good fit.

Energy Psychology

While acupuncture and acupressure have calmed and healed bodies for more than 5,000 years, psychological acupressure is just decades old. In these techniques, you touch or tap places on in your body—on Chinese meridians—while you focus on body sensations. Don't worry about getting the exact spots right as you start. Repeating phrases helps change your thoughts and emotional reactions.

Start by identifying the emotion and intensity, so you can compare your feelings at the end of the technique.

- In Callahan's **Thought Field Therapy** (TFT) or Craig's **Emotional Freedom Technique** (EFT) you tap—touch your fingertips like gently tapping a table—7 to10 times on the inner points of your brows, the sides of your eyes, under the eyes, middle of chin, under the inner collar bone, under your arms where a woman's bra would be, on your liver (4-6 inches under the right nipple). While you're tapping, you repeat a phrase such as, "Even though I have this _____ feeling, I fully and deeply accept myself."

- **Eye rolling.** TFT and EFT both have additional techniques that involve engaging the voice, logic, and rolling the eyes. Other eye-movement therapy techniques such as EMDR (Eye Movement Desensitization and Reprocessing) has effectively treated Post-Traumatic Stress Disorder. Rolling your eyes *slowly* in one direction, then the other, may help create release.

- **Tapas Acupressure Technique.** Gently touch your forehead with one hand and the bottom back of your head with the other. Repeat a phrase such as "I feel angry and I'm okay." Focus on the physical sensations as they get stronger and then abate. The touch on the head is a comforting support as the emotions release.

More information on these techniques and other psychological acupressure tools are on the Web at *http://www.tatlife.com*, *http://www.tftrx.com*, and *http://www.emofree.com*.

☆ Boosters: Body Alignment ☆

Evolution helped us stand up straighter—and get smarter. Theories abound that alignment supports the brain, reduces stress, eases emotions, and helps cognitive thinking.

When the body is tense, you trigger the "fight or flight" adrenaline response. Muscles compensate for misalignment, reducing blood flow to the brain. Research at the University of Leeds confirmed that bad posture can raise heart rate and blood pressure.

Alignment doesn't mean throwing your shoulders back and standing like a soldier in old cartoons. It means finding balance as you move.

Many ways help support the alignment of the body: Feldenkrais Method (movement reeducation to increase levels of vital energy), osteopathy (holistic medicine focusing on musculoskeletal alignment), chiropractic (spinal adjustment to improve bodily function), Rolfing (hands-on connective tissue manipulation), massage, yoga, Alexander Technique (teaching improved posture), ballet, Trager Approach (receptive and active body realignment), and others.

Some work on the bones, muscles, and tendons. Others are "somatic education," training the body to move differently. For instance, the Feldenkrais Method focuses on how the body is organized, using movement and self-awareness.

While you may want to visit a practitioner to expand your body's horizons, you can increase ability and awareness on your own. These boosters come from experience with Feldenkrais, yoga, and other practitioners, as well as the information from Dr. Pat Ogden, a pioneer in somatic psychotherapy.

- Notice places of relaxation, numbness, and tension in your body.

- Focus on one body part and play with how it moves. Are your shoulders independent of the chest? Does changing the tilt of the head affect the pelvis? Subtle shifts have large impact on the body.

- Observe the posture and movement patterns of others. Where do they lean or swerve when they walk? What parts are tense, smooth, or efficient?

- Imitate another walker. Notice how changing your alignment feels.

- How do you sit, drive, talk on the phone, and work on the computer? Does one side feel heavier, more tense, relaxed, or efficient?

- Notice how you balance when you stand. While the "perfect" posture shows the head-pelvis-and heels in line, bodies have idiosyncrasies and habits. Perhaps you tilt your pelvis to compensate for a head jutted forward (typical computer posture). Or you're a little twisted—if you look from above, your shoulders and hips make an X.

- Experiment with what posture allows you to breathe the fullest and easiest.

☆ Boosters: Move Your Brain ☆

In a favorite comic, Betty and her friend start off to run. "Exercise produces the feel-good hormone *end*-orphins," says Betty.

"Why doesn't exercise have *begin*-dorphins?" her friend whines.

You might feel resistance when starting to exercise, but once you're moving, the body is happier. It's common knowledge that exercise strengthens the heart, lungs, and muscles and increases your metabolic rate.

New information shows that exercise also makes your brain happier. That's because "movement is fundamental to the very existence of the brain," says Dr. John Ratey in *User's Guide to the Brain.* In fact, brains are found only in organisms that move from place to place.

> Exercise makes your brain happier. That's because "movement is fundamental to the very existence of the brain," says Dr. John Ratey.

Movement helps you think. The brain's cognitive and movement functions work side by side, sharing the same automatic process. When you solve a problem, you imagine moving through the steps. That's why you end up in the kitchen and forget what you're looking for—you remembered the action, not the item. In addition, exercise stimulates the production of brain chemicals, such as BDNF (brain-derived neurotrophic factor), which encourages growth of new nerve connections.

Women who walk regularly will be less prone to memory and cognitive loss. For every extra mile walked per week, said Dr. Kristine Yaffe at University of California in San Francisco, "there was a 13 percent less chance of cognitive decline."

Movement helps you feel better, too, by releasing those endorphins, among other hormones.

If you already exercise, keep going. The Centers for Disease Control recommend that adults should engage in **moderate**

intensity physical activity (increase in breathing and/or heart rate where you can still have a conversation) for at least 30 minutes on five or more days of the week. Or engage in **vigorous intensity** physical activity (large increase in breathing or heart rate where conversation is difficult or "broken") for 20-plus minutes on three or more days per week."

If you exercise reluctantly, add variety to reengage yourself. If you don't exercise, begin with a single step: park two blocks from the store and walk the distance. The invigoration and joy of movement will build over time.

What kind of exercise can you do? For your bones, strength, and balance, pump your muscles with weights, Gyrotonics (an exercise system to improve flexibility, balance, and muscle strength), yoga. For your heart rate, blood pressure, and endorphins, do some aerobic activity: running, walking, swimming—even rowing crew, ultimate Frisbee, and Parkour (a combination of gymnastics, running, and balance through park structures). Befriend your body and move. These suggestions may help.

- **Plan.** An exercise routine creates a pattern in your body and mind. Sign up for a class, schedule a walk with a friend, join a gym, and mark out time on your calendar. Get out your exercise clothes before you go to bed so you're dressed for a run first thing. Prepare for flexibility: keep your goggles, suit, and towel in the car.

- **Extend.** Add a challenge to each exercise. Do 5 minutes of quick intervals. Or fast-medium-slow intervals during your swim, run, walk, or bike. Shave a few seconds off the time of your regular route. Add just 5 more minutes. Walk a flight of stairs to work. If you haven't moved in a while, walk for 10 minutes each day, extending 5 minutes each week.

- **Snack.** Exercise "snacks" are great for newbies and anyone tethered to a computer all day. Pace on the phone or in your office. Catch a couple flights of stairs during a commercial break. Take a 2-minute walk to the mailbox or the Starbucks down the street instead of the one next door. Even a fast walk of 30 steps several times a day can rev you up.

- **Reward.** Monitor proof of exercise success. Put stickers on your calendar each day you've swum. Reward yourself with a new pair of shoes when you've reached a new goal, such as accruing 12 hours of exercise in a month.

- **Don't be bored.** Bring your mind with you as you exercise. Practice French. Say affirmations about how you're helping your body. Watch a video if you're at home. Listen to a book on your MP3 or to music, paced at the right rhythm for your movement. Then pop to a faster tune.

- **Build community.** Find others who support your exercise desires. Join with a friend to check in on your week's activity, get a personal trainer, even find support groups online at Yahoo, Google, and MSN.

- **Compete.** Join a team to engage in a whole routine of practices, games, and camaraderie—as well as a coach to guide the process. You can find teams for seniors, masters, or newbies at Craigslist, community centers, and gyms.

- **Coordinate.** Engage your thinking component as a part of moving with team sports, yoga, and dance (from jazz to ballroom).

☆ Boosters: Brain Exercise ☆

The leg bone is connected to the prefrontal cortex.

While exercise reinforces learning, you change how you learn with specific movement programs such as BrainDance and the BrainGym. They're taught to students, children, adults, dancers, and those with learning disabilities. BrainDance expands on patterns developed as babies that are "crucial to the wiring of our central nervous system," says Anne Green Gilbert, author of *Brain-Compatible Dance Education.* For instance, crawling and other cross-lateral movements help the brain develop readiness for reading.

Move in these areas a few minutes each day and before or during a break from learning.

- **Tactile sensations** spark neurons in the brain. Squeeze your arms, legs, head—the whole body. You can also tap, scratch, slap, and gently brush the skin as well. Try scratching your arms in a boring meeting.

- **Core-distal movement** reaches and curls the spine and limbs. Move from the center and extend through the fingers, toes, head, and tail. Then curl back while engaging core muscles, your abdominals. Repeat. Can be done standing or lying down.

- **Head to tail.** Wiggle and sway your head and tail (at the bottom of your spine) in different directions: forward, back, and side-to side. Keep knees bent for easier mobility.

- **Upper and lower body.** Move just your arms, head and torso. Then switch and move just the pelvis, legs, and feet.

- **Sides.** Make a big X with your arms and legs. Dance with the left side while keeping the right side still, then reverse and dance with the right side.

- **Cross-lateral.** Move so the opposite arm and foot move at the same time—crawl, skip, or swing your arms when you walk. For the Cross-Crawl, alternate touching one hand to opposite knee as if you were marching.

- **Vestibular.** Get dizzy by swinging, tipping, swaying, rocking, then reorient yourself with a few deep breaths.

Exercises to Open the Brain

These exercises are good for relaxation, focus, and learning.

- **The Hook-Up** is a twisty and calming move. Sit or stand with your ankles crossed. Extend your arms and cross your wrists; turn your hands so your palms face each other and clasp your hands (like a handshake). Bend your elbows so your clasped hands turn under and in towards your body. Rest your hands on your heart and breathe. Then uncross feet and place them flat on floor. Uncross arms and place your hands so fingertips touch opposite fingertips, thumbs pointing toward your heart. Breathe gently for approximately 30 seconds, and release.
- In the **Lazy Eight,** connect the two hemispheres of your brain by making the figure 8, first to the upper left and then the upper right. Use each hand separately, then both together. This simple move requires a little brain coordination.

- **Eye tracking** helps you focus and read. Follow the movement of your thumb with your eyes (not your head) as it moves back and forth to develop horizontal eye tracking. Then practice tracking up and down for the vertical.

☆ Boosters: Stress ☆

The brain needs stress—a certain amount. You create new synaptic connections when you learn a new language, develop a new habit, and find gifts in disappointments.

But for most of us, the word *stress* doesn't mean the good stuff. It means feeling strangled by time crunch, debt, noise, smog, cell phones, and conflicting desires of kids, spouse, boss, and yourself. That stress wears on the brain.

You need a balance of tension and relaxation. Or, in brain-talk, you need both the sympathetic and parasympathetic functions.

The *sympathetic nervous system* (SNS) turns on the stress response, preparing you to deal with perceived threats—fight or flight. The body releases adrenaline and cortisol hormones, which increase breathing, heart rate, and blood pressure. SNS puts other body systems, such as sexual function and the immune system, on hold. Even your blood-brain barrier is less effective at shielding your neurons from some poisons, viruses, and toxins. To top it all off, the SNS turns on more easily than it turns off, in case the threat returns.

The SNS body response is not good long term. The brain and memory are adversely affected by oversecretion of stress hormones from our time-crunch-noise-cell-phone-24-hour-news scene.

Fortunately, the *parasympathetic nervous system* (PNS) calms the body. Its function is to rest and digest. PNS hormones suppress the release of cortisol and gather up its remains in your brain; lower the heart rate and blood pressure; and reengage the digestive system.

Here are some boosters to help you can manage and flow with inevitable stress.

- **Reduce stressors.** Turn off electronics and other items that demand your attention. Take a news break. Make things quiet by closing the doors, going to a library, or turning on a fan. Get help dealing with stressful areas through a support group, life coach, therapist, career counselor, pastor, or friend. Or use books (I call it bibliotherapy). Take a break with a no-work personal "sabbath." Go on a vacation or spend time away from home to reduce stimulation.

- **Divert stressful energy.** Make use of stress hormones. Exercise, garden, build something, be sexual, pound a pillow, sing, clean the junk by the back door, walk around the block, cry, tap your feet, or write a letter.

- **Increase calm.** Focus on your body with a massage, bath, or spa visit. Exhale all the air from your lungs and bronchioles, and let the next breath come to you. Find an energy practitioner or do your own energy medicine (touch techniques, such as EFT and Tapas Acupressure Technique, that enhance flow in Eastern medicine's meridians). Meditate. Massage your own hands. Take a nap. Drink water. Try biofeedback, a technique that allows you to have some voluntary control over autonomic body functions, such as muscle tension, temperature, and blood pressure. There's a computer biofeedback game called Wild Divine—pretty fun. Do yoga. Drink tea. Connect with your deeper wisdom.

☆ Boosters: Lovely Lullabies ☆

Did you cuddle between your sheets, turn off the light, and snooze for seven to eight hours last night? About half of you reading this did.

For the rest of you, a full night's sleep is elusive. Perhaps you put sleep on the back burner because you're stressed for time. Or you drank too much coffee. Maybe you were awakened by a baby, snoring spouse, or overactive bladder. Illnesses from colds to fibromyalgia and hormonal changes interrupt sleep, as do medicines from antidepressants to steroids. Disorders such as sleep apnea (snoring that blocks the air passage), restless legs, and the ever-so-common insomnia can hinder the deep slumber you crave.

I know insomnia—in fact, I developed a program called *Restful Insomnia* to help renew during sleepless hours. Still, I like to sleep. In fact, sleep deprivation is the most common mental dysfunction.

When you don't sleep well, your memory, learning, coordination, even your creativity degrade. Sleep-restricted individuals have impaired memory and cognitive function, a shorter attention span, and a longer reaction time—possibly mimicking the symptoms of attention deficit disorder (ADD). The brain's natural neurogenesis (growth of neurons) is reduced. Significant sleep debt increases the symptoms of aging such as diabetes, hypertension, and obesity, said Dr. Eve Van Cauter of the University of Chicago. And sleep deprivation brings emotional and psychic havoc.

When you don't sleep well, your memory, learning, coordination, even your creativity degrade.

Sleep is manna from the night. It enhances brain connections (*neuroplasticity*), helping you learn information and processes, such as playing a musical instrument. Experiences get filtered to long-term memory. Have a tricky decision? Your brain reorganizes information when you "sleep on it."

Sleep connects you to natural body rhythms, though you may have to wrest yourself away from electronic, light-filled life at first. Try these tips to get more rest and check with a doctor or other resources (such as *RestfulInsomnia.com* or *Sleepnet.com*) if you need more help in renewing your brain with sleep.

- **Use the day wisely.** Go outside soon after awakening to set your body clock. Limit caffeine and alcohol. Don't smoke. Exercise—but not late in the evening. Keep a regular schedule of sleep and wake.

- **Create a cocoon** for sleep and rest. Get a comfortable bed—with a return guarantee to make sure the new one works. Clear the clutter so you won't think of folding clothes in the middle of the night. Put the television in another room. Use a "white noise" machine or fan to reduce the intensity of outside sounds. Open a window for ventilation. Turn your clock away. Keep it dark with curtains or an eye mask.

- **Put yourself to bed.** Create an "evening ritual" before bed: play soothing music, stretch gently, dim the lights. Increase production of melatonin by turning off the television or computer (stimulating, moving lights increase insomnia). Try a light bedtime snack:

herbal tea, warm milk, or foods with the amino acid tryptophan (milk, turkey, and peanuts) on an empty stomach. Avoid over-the-counter sleep aids, which may not be effective or may cause daytime drowsiness. Minimize use of prescription sleep aids. Read a neutral book to engage the unconscious mind. Write down what you're grateful for.

- **Return to sleep.** If you awaken in the middle of the night, let yourself rest. Keep it dark and quiet, even in the halls when you go to the bathroom. Put on an eye mask to create more darkness. If you read, use a book lamp. Meditate. Don't do anything stimulating, such as watching TV or using the computer. Focus on the sensations in your body, even those caused by emotions.

☆ Boosters: Visualization ☆

Ever wake and feel like your dream of landing a flying building was real? That's because your heart rate, breathing, and blood pressure all increased while you were dreaming. You might have even—like my husband did—called out to traffic control in the middle of your rapid eye movement (REM).

You don't need sleep to affect your mind with images. You can "create dreams" or visualizations during the day. They increase calm, change hormones, and even speed healing of wounds.

One form of visualization is hypnosis: you hear images that relax you, change beliefs, reduce triggers for unhealthy habits, and support healing.

You can work with a hypnotherapist, and you can give images to yourself. Here are some guidelines and alternatives to get you started, based on my training in Ericksonian hypnosis (therapeutic conversational hypnosis developed by Dr. Milton Erickson). You can find out more information from Shakti Gawain's *Creative Visualization* and other books on imagery and self-hypnosis.

- **Relax.** Slow your body down to engage the calming parasympathetic nervous system. If your mind is racing, focus letting the muscles relax from head to toe. Meditation techniques may help.

- **Uncover an intention.** You may be clear about the purpose of the visualization at the start. *Clear the congestion from my sinuses.* Or let the purpose of the visualization unfold. *Relax the tension in my head.*

- **Specify an outcome.** That is, state your intention as what you want from the visualization. *Get rid of my headache* isn't as clear to the body-mind as *relax my jaw.*

- **Create a healing place.** Imagine a beautiful place, perhaps in nature. Notice all the senses: images, sound, smell, touch, taste. See yourself becoming whole, healthy, and happy.

- **Move to healing.** Imagine moving toward a healing place rather than making a perfect image. Or visualize healing helpers to aid the process. The helpers don't have to be people: even healing mud can take away pain.

- **Engage the body.** See and feel your cells healing you, your immune system fighting the unhealthy invaders, tiny elves washing away the sinus infection with a hose spraying cleansing bubbles.

You can also read aloud from a self-hypnosis or visualization book. Or make a recording as you read the script or your own visualization. Play it back as you rest in a comfortable spot.

☆ Boosters: Light and Darkness ☆

We need light. And not just that fluorescent tube flickering above the cubicle. The brain uses light to enhance alertness. Even ambient light positively influences hormone release and heart rate, discovered researchers in Belgium and England.

Changes in light, from seasons to jetlag, affect the brain. Wintertime gray can lead to the blues, otherwise known as seasonal affective disorder. When the time changes (back and forth from Daylight Savings to Standard Time), there are more accidents on the roads. Time changes in the fall, when you gain an hour of sleep, are still hard on the body, says Professor Elliot Albers, advisor to NASA's National Space Biomedical Research Institute.

We need darkness as well, he says. It synchronizes your body clock. Problem is, there's too much light from lamps, computers, and television—even the haze of street lamps.

To increase the balance of light in your life:

- **Go outside,** especially in the morning. Go for a walk—even for a few minutes—before stepping into your office for the day.
- **Use light boxes in the winter.** My sister put hers on the breakfast table, or you can have one that shines when the alarm clock rings. Even a brief (20 minute) morning exposure to the sun or bright white light significantly boosts various areas of the brain, including your hearing!
- **Turn off or dim the television and computer.** Melatonin is the hormone produced by the pituitary gland and increases the body's natural rest and relaxation. Movement and bright lights inhibit your rest at night by diminishing production of melatonin.
- **Create dusk.** Help your body move to rest by darkening many rooms of your house at dusk.

- **Get dark at night.** Put in dark blinds or shades or use a good eyeshade to keep it dark when you sleep.

☆ Boosters: Color and Memory ☆

Feeling blue? Have a bright idea? Are you so mad, you see red?

Color is not just a little extra. It changes reality—even more than when Dorothy and Toto landed in Oz. Color helps you learn and remember, and it affects your awareness and even emotions.

Color alters the level of alertness, measured by alpha brain-wave activity (alpha rhythms reflect increased subconscious brain activity, often shown in meditation). In addition, says researcher Kathie Engelbrecht, when color is transmitted through the eye, the hypothalamus (the area of the brain that controls body functions) releases hormones that affect our moods, mental clarity, and energy level. That's probably why we feel better on sunny days.

Color helps you recognize objects, shapes, and natural scenes. A blue banana might work in a picture by Picasso, but not in the grocery store's produce section. By tagging color with shape, you process, store, and remember images more efficiently than if they're black and white. "Color information does not flow as a single stream from the eyes to the brain's visual area; rather, it takes parallel paths to other regions that process motion, shape, and texture," says Patrick Cavanagh, a Harvard professor of psychology.

On top of that, the color map in your brain (behind and below your temples) abuts the part that recognizes faces. So individuals with brain injuries who can't recognize their mother's face often can't see color either. The whole world is black and white.

Grey rooms don't help with studying, since the color of your environment affects how well you learn and focus. The U.S. Navy found that the frequency of accidents dropped 28 percent during the three years after they introduced color into the work environment.

Color also affects moods, and some color therapists believe it affects your body and health (*chromatherapy*). They may be right, since color lowered the blood pressure and changed the aggression of severally handicapped and behaviorally disturbed eight- to eleven-year-olds—including blind ones. The vibrations of color wavelengths may impact more than just our eyes.

Here are some methods of how color can enliven the brain:

- **Relieve eye fatigue and stress** by improving color and appropriate contrast. Add warm colors (yellow tones) to increase brain activity and body awareness. Or paint the wall that you look at when you take a break from your work; chose a medium tone, contrasting with lighter side walls. Studies show that distracting color combinations can slow reaction time and lead to task confusion.

- **Want to relax?** Lower the lights and pick cool colors (blue tones) to relax muscles and facilitate sleep.

- **Creativity.** To overcome writer's block, write or type in color, says consultant Mark Tillson, to engage both the technical and creative hemispheres of the brain. If you want to free-write on the computer (without your inner editor correcting every sentence) change the font color to pale yellow. Creative people may also have *synesthesia*, a condition in which they see colors for objects like numbers and letters. Check out more in chapter 3 on intelligence and learning styles.

Change Your Mood

Colors affect mood, say color experts, with its link to nature—soothing green of growth and the intense red of blood. You can use clothes to affect your mood or that of others. Paint walls or display art with colors that rev you up or soothe you.

- *Red* causes the heart to beat faster, makes you hungry, and prompts you to eat faster.
- *Blue* recedes, so objects appear farther away. It is the color of calm . . . or depression. Most police uniforms are blue, as in true blue.
- *Green* is the most restful color for the eyes. It helps people feel calm in schools or hospitals.
- *Yellow* is the most visible color of the spectrum. You'll see it on taxis, school buses, but rarely in fashion.

☆ Boosters: Senses ☆

Enhancing awareness of your senses positively impacts the brain—some consider sensory systems as the "windows to the brain." Here are some ideas to enhance sensual awareness.

- **Touch.** Get a foot rub, put an acupressure insole in your shoe that presses on reflexology spots, rub your hands together, scratch your scalp, walk barefoot, put your feet in cold water, or squeeze, tap, slap your skin.
- **Smell.** Aromatherapy is touted to reduce anxiety and increase learning, though research has not yet

measured all the claims. However, a study on healthy adults in England showed that lavender oil had a relaxing affect and rosemary oil significantly enhanced memory factors.

- **Taste.** Anticipate taste by noticing smell and colors before you bite in. Take one small sip or nibble—even one raisin or one M&M. Compare the taste to something else. Is it more sour than a pickle? Tangier than a jalapeño?

- **Sound and music.** Music soothes the brain. Music that you like activates the higher thinking centers in the brain's cortex. It also stimulates the brain's circuitry of reward and motivation, a part that also governs hunger, thirst, and sex. You respond physically to music, which is why slow music is restful. Beyond the beat and flow of music, spend time just listening to sounds. Start with those far away, then tune your ear closer and closer. Listen to silence or quiet between sounds. Sing. Notice dialogue—the timbre and rhythm of voices as well as the content—on buses or in coffee shops.

- **Sight.** Go to a gallery or art exhibit. Draw or do needlecraft. Find a view and see how far you can pick out details. Examine your sweater or the grain of the wood table for details. Paint a wall or change the image of your screensaver.

- **Balance.** It's not one of the five primary senses, but you need it to align the body in the world. See how it feels when you lean to one side, forward, or back in your everyday posture. Stand on one foot (near a wall if you'd like support) and notice how your weight shifts—extend the free leg forward or back. Stretch your limits of comfort a little bit; it helps your brain work. Ride a bike or balance on a curb like a kid.

Use Your Body-Mind

When Barbara lost her keys, her body was operating one way while her mind was on another track. Sitting for a moment and letting her senses and thoughts work together would bring a calm—and perhaps more successful—search.

Appreciate your body-mind as much as possible. It widens your brain.

3

Hey, Genius!

Intelligence, Memory, Learning Styles, and Creativity

Most are born geniuses and just get de-geniused rapidly.

—Buckminster Fuller

Michael's spelling was so bad, his contraction for I am was *I'me*. Multiplying by a number greater than two put him in a tailspin. He failed first grade, the nuns hit him with a ruler, and his father hit his head with his signet ring when he didn't know his homework.

No question, Michael was stupid—he told me so. He was scared to attend community college, stayed in entry-level jobs, and didn't think he could pass nursing school.

Michael also happened to be a master at decorating, a creative abstract painter, and a reader of everything from *Jane Eyre* to an encyclopedia on herbology. He could organize a legal office of 100 lawyers, give a psychic reading to stand your hair on end, and invent the best cookie recipes you've ever tasted.

Did I tell you he was stupid?

After a few years—about thirty—Michael dispelled the old vision of himself. He graduated with honors from a strenuous massage school, acing anatomy, physiology, and accounting for business.

If you feel dumb, uncreative, or incapable of "too hard" tasks (dancing, math, drawing, writing), you may distort your true ability to learn. Your hidden brilliance is still there, even if you didn't break 900 on your SATs. Discover how to strengthen your brain by tapping into your multiple intelligences, learning processes, and creativity.

More Than One Kind of Smart

Hallie struggled with school. She had a hard time remembering facts and made little progress with writing or spelling. Despite her difficulties, she knew how to connect with others. She "embodied hope" said her second grade teacher. Through Hallie, her teacher learned about smarts beyond the curriculum.

Hallie had what Dr. Howard Gardner calls "interpersonal intelligence." Dr. Gardner developed the theory of multiple intelligences, going beyond the IQ test to discover the many ways humans are smart. He established criteria such as case studies, specialized brain functions, and evolution. Then he identified intelligent abilities including language, music, spatial reference, kinesthesia, naturalistic, and possibly existential intelligence.

These definitions by Dr. Gardner include ways to improve your weaker areas—strengthening your brain. Learning—even about learning—reduces risk of developing Alzheimer's, says the American Academy of Neurology.

If you're curious about your intelligence strengths, assess them at *http://www.ldrc.ca/projects/miinventory/miinventory.php* or other Web sites.

Gardner's Multiple Intelligences

- **Linguistic intelligence** reflects ability to read, write, tell stories, and learn languages, grammar, and syntax. Strengthen this ability by studying a new language, improving vocabulary (try Word-of-the-Day emails or *www.freerice.com*), and writing.

- Your friendly computer programmer has **logical-mathematical intelligence**. She's at home with numbers, logic, reasoning, and abstractions. To increase logical ability, get a book of logic games, knit a sweater, and learn computer programming. Or watch a movie on video—then stop it to predict what will happen.

- Those who have a high level of **musical intelligence** are sensitive to sounds, tones, rhythms, pitch, musical keys, and structure of the songs (from verse and chorus to symphonies). Borrow different types of music CDs, sing with the radio, be quiet and listen to the sounds around you.

- Those with strong **spatial intelligence** can imagine, understand, and represent the visual-spatial world. They may have a good sense of direction, hand-eye coordination, and visual memory. My mother, for instance, can visualize how furniture fits in a room without measurements. She can also buy a scarf that matches the blue in a blouse at home—perfect "chromatic pitch." To strengthen your spatial intelligence, be a backseat driver and provide directions for a trip, fit the groceries in the bag or the car, play with jigsaw puzzles and mazes, build some Legos, or sculpt some clay.

- Remember Gene Kelly performing "Gotta Dance!" in *Singing in the Rain?* He had **bodily-kinesthetic intelligence**, as do athletes, builders, actors, or surgeons (if they have fine motor skills). Yoga is great way to increase this ability. Make crafts or build, ride a bike, dance, and learn tai chi or other sports.

- Someone with **interpersonal intelligence** is good at organizing people and is aware of moods and motivations. He or she can communicate and lead well. To get more people skills, practice active listening—that is, repeat back what you think someone said. Learn about the types of personalities with the Myers-Briggs test (psychological preferences such as extraversion and introversion) or the Enneagram (a theory of nine personality types—possibly centuries old). Check the Internet for information, including *www.myersbriggs.org* and *www.enneagraminstitute.com.*

- **Intrapersonal intelligence** is the ability to be self-aware and explore emotions, goals, and motivations. This perspective on the human condition is used by writers, philosophers, psychologists, and theologians. To improve your intrapersonal intelligence, "know thyself"—write in a journal, meditate, try the personality tests mentioned above.

- Individuals with green thumbs and "horse whisperers" have **naturalistic intelligence.** They are sensitive to nature and may easily recognize and classify species. To get more naturalistic intelligence, expose yourself to the great outdoors: plant a seed, volunteer at an animal shelter, take a walk with a naturalist at the park, read about classifications of animals (kids books can be a great place to start).

- **Spiritual or existential intelligence** fits all Dr. Gardner's criteria except for association with a specific brain specialization—though this intelligence could be a whole-brain function. Those with this ability explore questions about life, death, and what lies beyond the subjective perspective. Prayer and meditation increase whole-brain communication and lessen the blood flow to the parietal lobes (which give a subjective sense of time and space). Explore what lies beyond thought through inquiry, reading, or talking with others.

Your intelligence reflects how your brain **computes** information, says Dr. Gardner. Meanwhile, how you **get** new information reflects your learning style. You'll likely find that learning is easier when you know how you learn.

The Fragrance of Learning

We would still have a closet-sized kitchen in our house if a computer programmer hadn't invented three-dimensional design software.

I wanted to expand a few feet so we could open a cupboard door and the oven at the same time. My husband didn't object exactly, he just couldn't understand what I wanted. It didn't matter if I drew pictures, put Post-it notes on the floor, or compared it to his sister's kitchen.

My husband is a verbal man—he learns by reading, listening, and thinking. Visualizing for him is like basketball star Michael Jordan hitting .300 in baseball. Not easy.

Thank goodness for the software! I laid out the dimensions of the kitchen on the computer and he could virtually walk through the room. All of a sudden the remodel was a great idea (especially now that it's done).

We all have learning styles that utilize specific senses that make learning real for your brain. Did you memorize the Gettysburg Address? It's just words until you hear the poetry, imagine Lincoln speaking, or feel the suffering of *the brave men who struggled here.*

Hearing poetry is the *auditory* learning style. Imagining Lincoln is the *visual* style. Feeling the suffering is the *kinesthetic* style that notices physical perception and movement. These are the primary learning styles. Some people also use the sense of smell and taste in learning. Most people favor one mode, even if they're capable in several. I learned about these styles when studying neurolinguistic programming (NLP), an approach to improve external and internal communication, though they're used in many models.

How do you know which style is yours? Start with your everyday words.

My son gives a good example. I asked him to describe a medical procedure he had as a child: "Tom Chapin music was on the head set, the doctor talked, and she used a long thingy to make a loud scraping sound in my ear." Guess what? He's auditory, just like his dad. My daughter described a field trip: "The bus was bouncy and took forever, then we climbed the ropes course and crowded around the tide pools." She's kinesthetic.

Check out your own style by writing a description of an event. See how your words match these descriptions.

People who are strong **visual** learners experience life in images. They picture options and remodeling plans. When something works, it *sheds light.* When something is plain, it's *lackluster* or *blank.* They *imagine* ideas, want to *point out* plans, and think an insensitive person is *blind* to reality. Visual processors often use pointing gestures.

Auditory learners experience the sounds of life—from verbal instructions, music, and reading. Some focus internally on their thoughts and concepts. When auditory processors describe something that works, it *rings a bell* or *resonates.* When something is plain, it's *flat* or *muted.* They *recall* ideas, want to *talk though* plans, and think that insensitive guy is *deaf.* Auditory processors may keep the head tilted to listen better.

Kinesthetic learners experience feeling, touch, and movement. They tune into the body to understand (a slower and deep way to process information). They describe that something *vibrates* or *strikes them* if it works. Something plain is *dull.* They *get a hold* of ideas, *move through* or *direct* plans, and think an insensitive gal is *numb* or *unfeeling.* Kinesthetic processors may touch your arm or their own as they talk.

Someone who *smells a rat* or says their day was *yummy* processes using the **gustatory** (taste) or **olfactory** (smell) senses.

Increase Your Learning Senses

If you want to experience more sensations, process ideas differently, and communicate better with others, practice new learning styles.

Respond to customers with their natural mode: if she *hears what you're saying,* close the deal by *listening to her ideas* rather than *pointing out new features.* When you use more of your brain, says NLP trainer Ragini Michaels, you become more flexible and better able to navigate the world.

Sensate Learning

Check out these learning style brain boosters.

- **Remember a scene,** say, cooking dinner, and engage all the sensual modes. Notice the colors on the cutting board, the taste of the sauce, the sound and smell of onions sautéing, the movement to cut the carrots.
- **Create a scene in your mind** with your primary style. Then enhance with your weaker area. For visual ability, imagine a picture or a movie of it. Add or subtract details, such as color or black-and-white to get an image that works. For kinesthetic ability, notice the feel on your skin (rough sand, wind on your face), temperature, movement, and feelings that arise. For auditory ability, imagine sounds (waves, seagulls, families talking) and your thoughts.
- **Translate words** into different modalities. Say "Hello" using taste ("What's cooking?"), kinesthesia ("How are you feeling?"), vision ("Beautiful day!"), and auditory ("Glad to talk with you"). Try phrases for good-byes ("See you later"), ignoring ("tuning out"), and attitudes ("taking a stance").
- **Echo others.** Try out the learning styles of friends and colleagues. Echo a word, gesture, eye movement, or stance. (It's a good way to establish rapport, if you're subtle and don't mock the other person.) Point upward,

talk quickly, and mention *lighting up* at a concert—that's the body's visual learning style.

By practicing new learning styles and multiple intelligences, you expand the brain. You also change habits. That's a key for creativity.

☆ Boosters: Brain Allies ☆

When you learn Sudoku or do the Sunday *New York Times* Anacrostic puzzle, you're engaged in the same process: introducing familiar pathways to new neurons. At first you might feel your brain stretch, feeling a little awkward or stupid. Then you begin to enjoy the challenge.

You move through two stages to learn a skill, according to Dr. Ratey, author of *A User's Guide to the Brain.* At first, cells receive stimulation through attention or movement. In the next stage—practice—you refine and add neurons to the neural pathways. You can see this with learning to play an instrument: cells are stimulated as you listen for sounds, read music, and move your fingers from C-major to G-minor. With practice, the song changes from *plunk-plunk* to music. Then you know the song without looking—a deepened neuropathway from a changed brain.

Creating challenges in everyday experience is the best road to make more neurons available for learning. Crossword puzzles and other abstract mental challenges are a good start, according to experts on aging at the University of California. People who did crossword puzzles four or more times a week nearly halved their risk of developing Alzheimer's disease.

However, disease prevention isn't the only purpose for challenging your brain. When you have joy in learning—doing what intrigues, amuses, and interests you—you'll do it longer, engage body senses, and keep your brain fluid and functioning. Not to mention having fun.

Support the Successful Brain

Be gentle, since a stressed brain doesn't work or remember as well. A psychology study divided a class into two sections for a test: one had the hard questions first, the other had easy ones first. Guess who got better grades? Yep, the ones who started with the easy questions. Your brain likes success, so build it in as you challenge yourself.

- **Try something new.** Visit a new place, learn a song, rearrange the furniture—they all stimulate your neurons. Take up quilting, learn bridge, or enroll in community classes in engine repair. Even if you're an old dog, you can learn new tricks.

- **Do normal things in odd ways.** Brush your teeth with your left hand, if that's the nondominant one. Take a new route home. Sleep on the wrong side of bed. Lean over and look at the ocean upside-down through your legs (one of the most naturally weird things I've ever done). Your brain builds new neuro-pathways from familiar ones.

- **Have a context** for learning. When my well-educated sister has a paper to write, she checks out children's books on the topic before she starts her adult research. The easy-to-read summary of Shakespeare's plays makes learning the history of *Much Ado about Nothing* much smoother.

- **Use your body senses.** Renna, who retrained her brain after a car accident, helped her recovery by paying attention to cooking. She noticed the color of veggies, smell of spices, and texture of food. She made cloth dolls, relishing the touch and colors of the fabric and manipulating it with her hands. "Focus on colors and the pull of the yarn as you knit," she says, because sensory stimulation engages the brain.

- **Heighten your sensual experience.** Get dressed with your eyes closed (engage your touch, smell, movement, and hearing). Can you make sense of the Braille buttons on the elevator? Listen to sounds as you sit for 5 minutes—the distant plane, lawn mower, refrigerator humming, cat's purr, breathing.

- **Take a break** from your cell phone, computer, TV, radio, Gameboy, TiVo, iPod, personal digital assistant, and digital camera. You may be bored at first, but that's like being thirsty. Your brain wants to be engaged, not just entertained.

- **Play** with others as you learn. Ballroom dancing was shown by the Einstein Aging Study to keep the brain alive and well. Even thumb wrestling or a game of gin rummy helps your brain stay agile.

- **Ask questions.** Parents of "gifted" children encourage learning with streams of questions. "How do they put toothpaste in the tube?" Be inquisitive alone or with friends. Curiosity will stimulate your thinking brain, says Dr. Daniel Amen of *Making a Good Brain Great.*

- **Compare.** Dr. Amen suggests you compare similar things, such as various paintings of the ocean or baseball batting stances to notice similarities and differences.

- As mentioned earlier, **movement** helps learning, since the brain's cerebellum coordinates movement of the body and thoughts. Crawling strengthens kids' ability to read. Even mouthing words can help learn a language. Physical actions—walking, talking aloud, or even driving—activate numerous motor centers to support cognitive functions. And exercise, of course, pumps blood and nutrients to the brain and works your muscles and heart. Learning a skill like woodworking, aikido, or landscaping is a great combination of movement and brain challenge.

- **Memorize.** Adults in Ireland spent six weeks memorizing articles and poems. While results didn't show up immediately, six weeks later they had changes in the hippocampus (the memory engine of the brain) and showed clearer memory of words and recent events.

Dr. Amen adds more ideas: Dedicate 15 minutes a day to new learning; cross-train at work; improve skills you have; practice what you know; limit television and video games (they increase attention deficit disorder (ADD) and aggressive behavior); join a class or group that challenges you; identify and treat learning problems; and break routines.

☆ Boosters: Both Sides of the Brain ☆

Use both sides of your brain to engage the big picture and details. Crossword puzzles engage your abilities in language, images, memory of words, and logic. Make solving them fun, not a test, said Will Shortz, *New York Times* crossword puzzles editor. "Using dictionaries, maps and other references is not cheating. It's your puzzle."

Does the popular Sudoku engage the whole brain as much as crossword puzzles? I asked Dr. Eric Chudler, University of Washington bioengineering professor and developer of the Neuroscience for Kids Web site. He hadn't seen any data on brain activation for either puzzle, but guessed that the visual processing activates both hemispheres. However, memory functions (used more in crosswords) activate multiple areas of the brain.

Language and music embody complex, whole brain structures, as does writing. Try singing or humming while you learn. Einstein played violin for inspiration, stopping midpiece to write down his ideas. Expand your vocabulary with a "word-of-the-day" email, calendar, or through testing word knowledge at the hunger-support Web site, *www.freerice.com*. Get creative and stimulate your whole brain.

Both sides of the body engage both sides of the brain. Play a guitar, swing both arms as you walk, or do a yoga pose. Energy medicine teacher Donna Eden suggests you alternate tapping opposite elbow and knee—lift your right knee, touch it with your left elbow or hand, then reverse back and forth for a while. See chapter 2 for more movements that help the whole brain engage.

Forget to Remember

Forgetting is a good thing.

Yes, it's awkward to forget the name of a former client or the milk at the store. And nobody wants to get Alzheimer's—forgetting the names of loved ones.

Still, do you really want to remember what you had for dinner on Wednesday . . . three weeks ago? We need to forget or "trivial moments would clog our minds," says Dr. John Ratey, author of *User's Guide to the Brain.*

Forgetting helps you focus. You filter attention to notice what's important (the book in your hands) and generalize everything else (the chair you're sitting on). When the brain is busy with TVs, cell phones, Blackberrys, and even stress, important information moves to the fringe of your awareness.

Remembering is a good thing, too.

Remembering and forgetting and remembering create learning. That helps you increase your brain's neurogenesis. As I mentioned in the chapter 1, you generate new neurons until you die. Learning also creates and strengthens neuropathways, making familiar habits stronger (like deepening the ruts on a cross-country path) and engaging less-used neurons (so you can ski in new locations).

Here are some factors involved in strengthening the memory:

- When you learn and remember, you use the **whole brain**: the two hemispheres of the cerebrum, primal brain stem, hypothalamic body regulators, limbic system, and thalamus.
- **Senses** are critical to your learning and memory, says Dr. Ratey. They store and access information, including our memory clues.
- **Emotions** affect learning. Neurons use neurotransmitters to transmit information; certain neurotransmitters, such as serotonin, norepinephrine, and dopamine, trigger emotions. It's harder to learn when you're anxious or upset.
- **Short-term memory** (working memory) is a temporary repository for learning. It can hold about seven pieces of information for 10–20 seconds. If you want to keep the information longer, transfer it to your long-term memory with focus or a learning technique.
- **Practice** deepens the neuropathways, which strengthens skills and habits.
- **Movement** is key to learning. When you think and plan, you imagine movement—you see yourself in a meeting or picking up groceries.

It would be great if you could turn on your learning brain, just like plugging in a 500-gigabyte computer. However, as humans, there are obstacles to learning and memory we can overcome.

When to Worry

The biggest fear for most people is Alzheimer's. In reality, only 10-15 percent of people ages 65 to 100 show its symptoms. How can you tell if you have a normal slip of the brain or dementia?

Normal aging memory decline is a tip-of-the-tongue search for words or names not often used (like someone you see once a year). Individuals with Alzheimer's or other senile dementia lose names for common objects such as a chair or spoon. They can't initiate the retrieval process, even if they have the memories, says Dr. Ratey. However, if you provide the beginning of a story or an image, they can pull the memory together with enough time.

Symptoms of Alzheimer's Disease

According to the Alzheimer's Association, these symptoms of senility appear on an ongoing basis, not on occasion as with depression or other health issues.

- Memory loss that can't be recalled later
- Difficulty performing familiar tasks
- Problems with language
- Inability to orient to time and place
- Poor or decreased judgment
- Problems with abstract thinking
- Misplacing things
- Changes in mood or behavior
- Changes in personality
- Loss of initiative

Worrying about learning decline is a stressor in itself. Instead, accelerate your learning and memory process by playing with the brain.

☆ Boosters: Challenge Your Memory ☆

"Don't I know you from somewhere?" I see vaguely familiar faces I might have met at prenatal yoga fifteen years ago or a baseball game last month. Someone might look familiar, but I can only identify her as "Ruthie's mom" instead of Anne.

I don't worry too much about forgetting names. I heard a radio story that said our brain had name-memory space for life in a village: about 200 people, herbs, animals, and tools. Now we're expected to remember the latest *Project Runway* contestants, new hybrid cars, and the author of a book we read in college. Add to that all the numbers to remember and blogs to read . . . it's no wonder we forget.

Remember Names

While I've stopped stressing at name memory, I appreciate the techniques that help me remember. I've classified four steps that encompass all the name-memory techniques I've seen: Practice, Sense, Associate, and Link.

1. **Practice.** Say the name aloud or mouth it when you're introduced and during the conversation. If you forget (easy to do if you're stressed or there's lots of other stimulation), confess your sins and repeat the name when your acquaintance tells it to you. If he has an unusual name, ask him to spell it—and repeat it back. The visual image of the name can help secure it.
2. **Sense.** Notice a physical characteristic—hair color, clothing, features—that help you distinguish the person so you can connect the name to the face. Pay attention to the context of where you're meeting as

well. The third time I met Jane in yoga, I noticed she always had a blonde ponytail, neat bangs, and brought a purple mat—and I don't forget her name.

3. **Associate.** Connect the name to something familiar. Remember others who have the same name. If you meet Davey at a party, remember your baby-sitter has the same name; you'll create a familiar "name file folder" instead of a new one for each person. If the person's last name reminds you of something physical—Carpenter—imagine her with a hammer. Or relate the sound of the name to an image: Valerie may bring to mind a valley; Stier may remind you of cattle. Rhymes help: Phil/pill, Anna/banana.

4. **Link.** Create an association chain with the name. Imagine a valley of cows in the hair of Valerie Stier. Link the name with something about the person. Franny may have frizzy hair; Hannah may use her hands when she talks. If you meet Fred Bender, imagine him leaning over to pick up something red.

Use Mnemonics

The word *mnemonics* is related to Mnemosyne, the Greek goddess of memory. Mnemonic techniques are memory tools—links to help recall difficult-to-remember information. The link or code can be a phrase ("Thirty days hath September"), letters, numbers, pictures, songs, or even an imagined journey.

Students use mnemonics to memorize history or anatomy. I use it when I can't write my shopping list while driving. The key is using vivid images and sensations to create strong association and recollection.

Here's an example: During dinner, my family remembered we needed to bring fabric paints and a pink baseball cap to a party (don't ask, there were good reasons). We used mnemonics to remember. We imagined a 5-foot fuchsia hat decorated with lime green fabric paint. We imagined the hat in the trunk of the car, almost too big to close the trunk lid.

This hat was linked both to the fabric paints and transportation (car). The image was huge—impossible to avoid if it were real. The mnemonic images were embedded in our mental preparations to leave. The next morning, as we packed the trunk, the image of the fuchsia baseball cap jostled our memories.

Making Mnemonics

To make your own mnemonics memorable, here are items suggested by *MindTools.com*:

- Use pleasant and positive images. You'll be drawn to remember them.

- Make your images vivid, colorful, and noticeable. Exaggerate the size of key parts of the image.
- Use all your senses. The hat could have had an alarm, been lush velvet, done a tap dance, or smiled. Use three dimensions and use movement—the hat could have driven the car.
- Be funny, peculiar, odd. If you make a poem or rhyme, be outlandish or even rude.
- Symbols such as traffic lights, road signs, fingers can code information. If you want to remember three things, one might be in the red light, one in the yellow, and one in the green.
- Place things on top of each other, crashing or merging into each other. They can rotate or dance. Items can talk to each other or to you.
- Use location to boost your memory: Put each shopping item on a chair in the living room, and then imagine you're walking through the room when you're in the store.

Creative Flashes

Creativity uses the whole brain. But it requires letting go of what you think should happen. I know from experience. I had a creative flash one Saturday. I spent an easy hour writing and then saved my document via laptop to our house network (creation of my computer-geek husband).

At 5:00 a.m. the next day I had another flash. Only it was an electrical transformer blowing up outside. The file was gone from the laptop, from the network, and from the searches my geeky husband did.

No big deal, I thought—just an hour's work. Problem was, when I started to rewrite, my creativity was blown. Instead of flow, I spent hours and hours in an obstacle course. My critic was in full gear, comparing each sentence with the imagined "must-have-been-better" vanished version. I chased my creative juices—they were like a mirage in the Sahara.

Chasing creativity is a common path for many of us. We think we need a special place, hours of time, or the best tools along the way. We insist on milestones (a remarkable painting, scientific theory, or Pillsbury Bake-Off prize) to prove we're headed in the right direction. Or we refuse to take a step, saying we're not creative enough; we compare ourselves to Albert Einstein, Winslow Homer, or J. K. Rowling.

The Path to New-Where

Does creativity reflect genius, or can we all engage in it? Is it an inner process or something tangible—a product? Do creative people need to be "masters in a domain" (as Dr. Gardner stated), or can we connect knowledge from different fields?

"Creativity," author and creativity coach Eric Maisel told me, "reflects our potential as humans. It creates meaning in your life." The more someone recognizes creativity, the more it flows, he said. He or she becomes aware of ideas, plays with them, and takes them further. It expresses our self, our consciousness, the essence of who we are, added NLP practitioner Ragini Michaels.

Creativity starts with inspiration—a novel idea that knocks *your* socks off. Who cares if it's old news to someone else? Inspiration isn't just a better mousetrap. You can be inspired about words, images, music, everyday problems, emotions, behavior, movement, and thoughts.

> Creativity reflects our potential as humans. It creates meaning in your life.

We get confused about whether "creative" means the inspiration or the product—or both. According to tales about Walt Disney, creativity involves three stages: dreamer, realist, and critic. If you want to create a huge stuffed flamingo for your backyard, you *dream* its details (50 feet tall with illuminated feathers), decide if it can *realistically* work (zoning restrictions), and hone the product with useful *criticism* (feathers look silly on the head).

People who criticize their ideas before they're cooked derail creative dreaming with judgments and comparisons. That's what I did while I rewrote my lost article, until I moved into the flow again, allowing the critic to move aside. When creativity flows, the juices knit the brains neurons together in a path to new-where.

Who Lays the Path?

For years, the right side of the brain hogged the creativity credit; scientists believed that it was the font of original ideas. However, recent functional brain scans show that the whole brain engages in problem solving and creative thinking through the associative cortex.

The associative cortex sits in the frontal, parietal, and temporal lobes (front, back, and middle) of your brain. It links your senses, emotions, logic, social abilities, language, skills, memories, movement, and thoughts in potentially novel ways. These connections can be used immediately or can be stored as part of the unconscious mind, says Dr. Nancy Andreasen in *The Creating Brain.*

You use your associative-creative brain every day, even if you don't envision the story of Harry Potter while stuck on a delayed train. Take reading: your associative brain creates the rumble of the train, the electrical transformer flash, the pen drawing Mickey Mouse. Even your talking is associative. When you describe a new movie, you remember sadness at Dumbledore's funeral, associate words into sentence, and gauge the interest of the person who's listening so it's not a monologue. It's an associative process each time, unless you parrot the same information.

Everyday associative processes are *ordinary creativity,* according to Dr. Andreasen. If you want to deepen to *extraordinary creativity,* you experience life from an altered framework. An altered state is different than your ordinary waking state. You let go of daily logic and open to new perceptions. You may experience altered states near sleep, playing music, relaxing in the shower, meditating, being aware of the present moment, dancing. Some call this state *flow* (focused concentration), *REST* (random episodic silent thought), or surrendering to the muse.

Some people naturally have odd or creative connections in their brain. Their senses "cross-talk" so that certain letters, notes of music, even names are associated with colors or tastes. For instance, two is yellow, three is blue, four is green (these are absolute facts in my mind). This cross-wiring is called *synesthesia,* and it is more common than was once thought. You may discover how your senses overlap when you pay attention to your mind.

Enjoying your sense of play, magic, and sensitivity helps you associate new neural pathways.

☆ Boosters: Creative Inspirations ☆

These creative boosters come from neuroscientists, writers, creativity coaches (especially the *Creativity Book* by Dr. Eric Maisel), and ordinary creative people.

Stoke the Creative Desire

Unleash creative joy in your busy life.

- **Get bored.** Expand your creativity when you reduce your entertainment—TV, Internet, computer and video games, even movies. Being entertained is passive. Boredom spurs you to create something new, from your own brain. "The life of the creative man is led, directed, and controlled by boredom," says cartoonist Saul Steinberg. In fact, he goes on, "avoiding boredom is one of our most important purposes." Or try a week of reading deprivation, suggests Julia Cameron. Emptying our lives of distractions, she says in *The Artist's Way,* actually fills the well for new connections.

- **Dive in.** Contrary to Julia Cameron's suggestion, many writers recommend that you read as much as possible in order to write. Artists may spend days in art museums, musicians keep their MP3 players plugged in, and quilters take breaks in fabric stores.

- **Make creativity part of your "religion."** Participation in the creative act, says Maisel, is a participation in the mystery of life. Using your "billions of neurons and own two hands" instill meaning in life.

- **Create a ritual.** Make creativity into a daily routine. Write each morning; repeat a phrase about your creativity ("I live a creative life"); spend 5 minutes imagining creative dreams; dance with paintbrushes . . . whatever moves you toward the new. Repeat your ritual for at least twenty-one days, even if you're bored or embarrassed at doing it. You'll change your relationship to creativity as the weeks pass.

- **Let your ritual go.** You don't need your ritual to create. Just like Dumbo the Elephant, you can fly without the feather.

- **Make a creative space,** suggests Ned Hermann, chair of the Whole Brain Corporation. Could be a studio or corner where you have easy access to your tools can work unfettered, display your products, and affirm your creativity. Post notes reminding the world—and yourself—that you are an "Artist in Residence."

- **Take yourself on a creative date.** Go alone to an art museum, suggests Cameron, or a craft store. Take a rendezvous with nature and let your associations flow.

- **Wait.** Your brain and creative system may need a little space to let your innovations emerge. You can't force creativity to happen, says Ragini Michaels. Relax, notice, and wait for it to surface.

- **Meditate.** Meditation increases creativity. Neurons connect more strongly, retrieve more memories, and generate links between disparate topics, reports Sharon Begley in her book *Train Your Mind, Change Your Brain.* Meditation can reduce anxiety and diminish emotional creative blocks, leaving more energy for creative work. (See chapter 8 on meditation for more information.)

Reroute the Critic

The critic has its time and place, but it can interfere in the dreaming stage.

- **Honor anxiety.** Anxiety arises because you break down your old way of looking at things (create chaos) and generate new order. Anxiety comes with creativity—that's competitive collaboration, says Michaels—but don't let it stop the process.

- **Talk back to anxiety—and let it go.** When you judge your creative effort, you set up obstacles and distort the truth. You might hide judgments behind comparisons or excuses ("I'm not inspired, I can't do it"). Acknowledge the feeling or excuse, says Maisel ("Part of me feels anxious . . ."), then answer back and continue creating (". . . and I can still tap into my creativity").

- **Write.** Hand-write three "Morning Pages" each day to unleash creativity, encourages Cameron. These stream-of-consciousness pages drain your brain of accumulated thoughts and let creative ideas emerge. It doesn't matter what you write, she says. Over time, the morning pages "pry loose some of [the critic's] power over your creativity."

- **Breathe into affirmations.** Affirmations are short, positive phrases that state the reality you want: *"I'm fine just as I am." "I can compose a moving poem."* They support new thinking and may help manifest an action. However, affirmations work better when your body feels the statement's truth, says counselor Narayana Granatelli. Remember a creative time, she says, and imagine having those same sensations when the affirmation comes true. In his *Ten Zen Seconds,* Eric Maisel suggests you say the affirmation as you take a 10-second breath. Exhale first, then inhale for 5 seconds as you say the beginning of the affirmation ("I am fine . . ."); say the rest of the affirmation (". . . just as I am") as you exhale for another 5 seconds.

- **Make a mistake.** The creators of the Hopi Indian tapestries always put a mistake in each one, so I've heard. I purposely make a mistake (okay, many of them) in the details of my embroidered needlepoint to quiet my perfectionist streak. It makes creating the piece more enjoyable—even if the rectangle leans a little to the right.

Get Up and Move

As mentioned earlier, the movement cortex of the brain is entwined with thinking and emotions. Movement helps unleash your mind, says Dr. Ratey of *User's Guide to the Brain.*

- People have more creative ideas after **exercise.** It clears the mind, raises energy, and improves mood for at least several hours afterward. A walk, run, or 25 minutes of aerobic activity frees your creative ideas. You might want to bring a small pencil and paper, though: Fred Lebow, founder of the New York City marathon, wrote his ideas in the dirt with a stick as he ran in Central Park until he could come back to copy them later.

- **Stretching** moves your brain and releases emotional blocks held in your shoulders, pelvis, or jaw. Stand tall and extend your arms behind you. Do a gentle yoga twist: sit or stand upright, then twist to the right, starting from your pelvis up your spine. Stretch your right arm out slightly and look toward that hand. Breathe! Return to neutral and do the other side. Try yoga to shake loose creative blocks.

- **Tap into your sexual energy.** Tune into creativity just like you tune into the body during sex. Notice each moment as you let go of the dishes, laundry, and critic. Step into your body's energy as you paint, write, or solve a problem.

- **Play a musical instrument** to get both sides of your brain working. Playing a song forces you to focus on the here and now, says Zazen Master Brad Warner.

- **Get up, get out of the house.** Connecting with nature—even if it's just in the garden—increases creativity, research shows. You leave details behind and see the bigger perspective on life as your inspiration germinates.

Let Go

Let go of old habits to discover new perspectives.

- **Step outside of your routine.** Visit a new place, write with your nondominant hand, or eat a fruit you've never tried.
- **Be eccentric.** "I hope I'm becoming more eccentric," says musician Tom Waits. "More room in the brain." Step back from rules about who you should be, and spice your life—and your thoughts. Put an odd bumper sticker on your car, collect thermometers, learn to yodel.
- **Surrender to your muse.** Give the muse or greater source a face. Ask for help from it and notice what you learn. Be led by its force instead of leading creativity in the direction you think it should go.

Make Time

How much time does it take to be creative? It takes an instant to come up with a new idea—though it may take a bit to disengage from mind chatter to hear it.

- **Start the day with creativity.** "When you express your creativity first thing," Eric Maisel told me, "you will already have sense of making meaning in your day." Our best thinking, he says, occurs in our dreams at night, which can be used for inspiration.

- **Be portable.** Carry a notebook to write ideas. Spend your free moments with a craft, sketch pad, or a notebook. Take pictures in your mind (or with a camera) and notice the designs around you.

- **Notice this moment** . . . and this one . . . and this one. . . . When you're not planning the future or worrying about the past, the newness of right here emerges. The present moment-ness is reflected in the creativity of musicians. They don't write a brand new song each time they get up on stage; they express the sound of each moment.

- **Take an hour.** Put a kitchen timer somewhere you can't see it moving, says Maisel, and set it for one hour. Sit. Do nothing: don't read, don't meditate, don't do yoga. You'll realize how long an hour can be. The next day, set the timer for an hour and do your creative project, sketches, dreams for what's emerging from your creative wellspring. You can get a lot done in an hour. Make a commitment to do this regularly.

- **Do the tiniest thing.** Anne Lamott of the book *Bird by Bird: Some Instructions on Writing and Life* suggests you focus on the "one-inch picture frame." That may be writing one small scene or memory, sketching the legs for your new dining room table, stitching a few beads onto your fabric, stopping to look at something new. Break a large project into chunks and move forward step by step.

Kindle Creative Thinking

Encourage creativity with imagination, questions, and associations.

- **Reframe the problem.** Einstein said, "Problems cannot be solved by the same level of thinking that created them." Look at the problem from new vantage points. For instance, imagine a problem solved. Or start a question with a different word—who, what, where, when, why, how. Take one solution and apply it to a totally different problem: How would you file your clothes instead of papers?

- **Stoke your imagination.** Be a kid and spark imagery. Shrink down and tour your blood vessels, lungs, or ear canals. Imagine a party for anyone from history—what would you serve to Shakespeare, Elvis Presley, and Mother Teresa? Make up a story about that oddly dressed woman in line: perhaps she's a spy, a retired astronaut, or a preschool teacher who stockpiled a million dollars.

- **Ask questions** even if you can't answer them. How do copy machines work? How many cells are in your fingernail? What if you were a firstborn instead of last? What sports would you play if you had superpowers like the Flash, Superman, or Elasti-girl?

- **Say "Yes."** Ever seen a performance by an improv theater group? One person says, "Let's go biking," another suggests biking to Asia, and soon the whole group has created a bridge of barges to cross the Pacific. It works because everyone said "yes." A *No* stops the creative energy, going back to square one. A *yes* moves you forward, allowing transformation and association to take place. Spend an hour or day saying *Yes* (or *Yes, and*) to everything. "Let's have boiled tongue for dinner," says your spouse. "Yes, and we'll serve it with pasta," you reply, "and keep the tongue on the side . . . for the dog."

Take Action

Making your project real adds joy and depth to your creativity.

- **Create a "crummy" first version.** Anne Lamott in *Bird by Bird* suggests you write a crummy first draft—though she uses different language to describe it.

- **Be productive.** Do something useful, even if it's not directly related to your creative project. Instill the creative sense in your regular work, to balance dreaminess and doing.

- **Produce a craft project.** Feel the tools in your hands with a simple needlepoint or birdhouse kit. Of course, you don't have to follow the directions—you can rip seams, add material, and start again.

- **Practice** piano scales, color mixing, embroidery samplers, stretching routines, and turning a symmetrical leg on your lathe. The more practiced and learned your skill, the more resources you'll have to innovate and create what you imagine.

- **Model others.** If you're stuck on *I can't,* imitate those who can. The brain will take hold of new attributes as you "act as if," say experts in NLP. Grab a brush and stand like Matisse might have. How did he pick his palette? Art students line the floors or

European art museums reproducing the masters to hone their techniques.

- **Imitate** the genius of others to spark your own work. Transfer art from one medium to another. I created a miniature version of Mark Rothko's canvas in beaded embroidery, learning more about his technique along the way. Writing teacher Priscilla Long, author of *Begin Again: The Portable Mentor for Practicing Writers* suggests you imitate "superlative sentences" from writers you admire. Use your own content with the same structure, diction (word type), verbs, nouns, adjectives, and emotional tone. This adds to your inner writing resources.

- **Find a creative community.** The most productive artists have a community, said Long. Find a writing meet-up, knitting group ("stitch and bitch"), painting class, choir, cabinetmakers happy hour, whatever. Or host your own. Look on the bulletin boards of coffee shops and community centers or online with Web sites like Craigslist.

Open the Doors

Michael's creativity opened the doors to his intelligence. He rediscovered math when he made an eight-foot macramé curtain in his hippie years. He learned to spell when he wrote poems. Once he healed these childhood misperceptions, he relished learning more: music, logic, dance.

Like we all do, he knows that there's always more to learn, though he appreciates how far he's come. When you take a moment to appreciate how you learn and create, you realize that you are already a genius in action. A genius with a working brain.

☆ Boosters: Brain Challenge Programs ☆

Challenge and stretch your cognitive thinking and sensory perception with brain exercises. There are lots of books, software, and kinesthetic programs that focus on brain exercise (see the Bibliography and Resources section). Start with these brain boosters to strengthen your mental muscle—do them alone or with others.

Number and Logic Games

- **Number Your Name.** Add up the letters of your name: Each letter of the alphabet equals its position (A = 1, B = 2, M = 13). You can keep adding until you get to a one-digit number. Henry would be 8 + 5 + 14 + 18 + 25 = 70. Then 7 + 0 = 7.

- **Sudoku** is a popular logic puzzle where you fill in missing numbers in a 9 by 9 square. Check the

Internet for tips, which help uncover patterns of logic. It's hard to correct a mistake in a Sudoku, but there's always a new one the next day.

- **Remember and Repeat Numbers.** Have someone read one row of numbers aloud, with a one-second pause between each. Repeat them in exact order. When that's easy, try repeating them backward.

1	4					
9	1	2				
2	9	5	4			
3	5	1	2	8		
7	8	2	6	5	1	
5	4	9	8	2	4	3

Movement Games

Have someone read these instructions for you to follow:

- Put your right hand on your left knee.
- Point to the floor after pointing to the ceiling.

Or play a game of Simon Says!

Word Games

Word games are great to play with family, while driving, or waiting for your waiter to come. I've played these games with people from age four to ninety-five.

- **Something Doesn't Belong.** One person names four or five items that form a group, except one item doesn't match. The others guess the wrong item and tell their logic. The correct answer has both the right item and right reason. Here's an example: *book, jump rope, movie,* and *knitting.* (My answer is *movie*—the only one that needs electricity. Someone else might guess *book,* the only one you read.)

- **Trailers.** Pick a category, for example, birds or items at a restaurant. One person names an item in the category. The next person names another item that starts with the last letter of the previous item. Animals could be *zebra, anteater, rhinoceros, spider, red ant.*

- **Words from License Plates.** This simple game is easy on a boring drive. Make words from the letters on license plates in the same order, trying for the shortest word. 787 PNS could be *princess* or *pins.* You can also make silly phrases—"Pumpkins Never Spit."

Curiosity for Brain Life

Your curiosity is the best sparkplug for learning, even if you forget all the boosters you've ever heard. Inquisitiveness keeps you aware of the world, connected to the wonders and mysteries of life.

When you keep learning, you stay young. "Anyone who stops learning is old, whether at twenty or eighty," said Henry Ford.

Exercise your mental muscles and dive into life.

4

Emotions and the Brain

When You Can't See the Forest for the Angst

Saying that men talk about baseball in order to avoid talking about their feelings is the same as saying that women talk about their feelings in order to avoid talking about baseball.

—Deborah Tannen

Marianne thinks she's in control of her rage—she doesn't break dishes or slam doors anymore. However when she screams about the stupid kids leaving the dirty dishes on the $#@&* table, her family quakes.

Her anger is justified, she thinks, because there's too damn much for her to do. Yelling breaks loose the tension (for an hour or so) and coerces the family to step up to the plate. But there's a price for her anger: everyone else is testy long after her meltdown ends.

While Marianne relishes her emotions—even negative ones—others may keep feelings in the safe-deposit box at the bank, where they don't have to look at them. No matter how you handle emotions, they reflect our relationship to life—to children, body, thoughts, food, work, even the commute home. They help to connect with people, make decisions, and understand oneself.

Emotions come in all shapes: negative, positive, and neutral. And they come in all sizes:

- *Feelings* come and go.
- *Moods* last a day or more.
- *Temperament* reflects emotional perspective.

Emotions help the brain quickly assess the world, communicate, and make decisions. However, emotions can run behavior and create an emotional stress cycle. They condition the mind to see from a narrow perspective. When you rage at someone you love or are too ashamed to take a risk in your career, emotions impinge on life.

Instead of being at the mercy of feelings ("I can't help that I yelled—I'm mad!"), transform emotional habits. The boosters at the end of the chapter can help change your relationship with emotions and create new pathways in the brain. Meanwhile, what are emotions, exactly?

> Instead of being at the mercy of feelings, transform emotional habits.

What Is This Feeling That I'm Feeling?

Remember the game you played at birthday parties, where the mom would stick a name on your back and you had to guess what it was? That game replicates the internal drama of emotional life. As an adult, you know you're feeling something—you stomach is quivery—but it could be excitement, fear, or even arousal. Defining emotions is like guessing what's on the back of your shirt.

Emotions are everywhere, visible and invisible, and can underlie physical, spiritual, philosophical, and cognitive perspectives. But basically, emotions are combinations of physical sensation, thoughts, and the urge for action.

Physical Sensation

Did the cat get your tongue? Is your stomach jittery from that scary movie? Your body changes with emotions, from the knot in the chest to changes in blood pressure, sweat levels, and muscle tension. Focusing on the *felt sense* of your emotion—heat in your rib cage, for example—helps interrupt an emotional stress cycle.

Thoughts

Emotions hang out with conscious and unconscious thoughts. In fact, some say there's no difference between emotions and thoughts, while others say thoughts come first. No matter what, you can enter emotions anywhere—thought, sensation, action—to make a change, says meditation teacher Sally Kempton.

Urge for Action

The word *emotion*—E-Motion—comes from the Latin word that means "to move." Actions may be involuntary: a smile, cry, or lowered eyebrows. Or they involve choice: a yell, pout, or cuddling the baby. "The function of emotions is to get us moving very quickly without having to think," says Charles Darwin.

Another function of emotions is to communicate with yourself and others.

If your stomach turns when you meet your sister's new fiancé, you know something's up. Exactly *what* is up may not be clear to you, even though others can tell that something's going on. Emotions are a universal language, according to pioneering researcher Paul Ekman. He brought pictures of people smiling, frowning, and grimacing to an isolated tribe in New Guinea. The tribe—living without the influence of televisions and movies—saw the same happiness, grief, and disgust as did other groups in the world.

Emotions are also key in making decisions. When a successful businessman had injuries affecting the part of his brain that governs emotion, it took him hours to decide where to eat. He analyzed the seating plan, menu, even management of restaurants. Emotions take precedence in the brain's wiring in decision making—intellect takes second place.

Emotional Wiring

Your emotional limbic system is about the size of a fist in the middle of your head. (See Figure 4.1.) It consists of many organs (such as the amygdala and hippocampus) and is in continuous communication with the logical and rational cortices. It is wrapped around the brain's movement system and sits just above the brainstem and spinal cord.

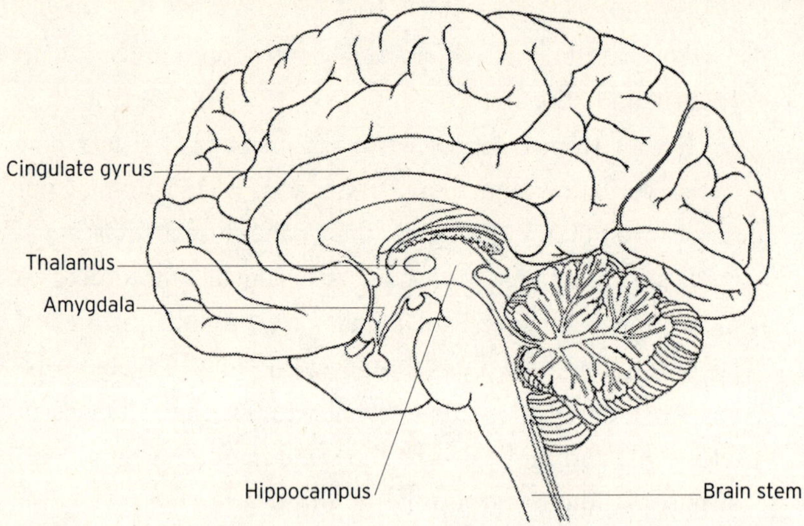

Figure 4.1. The limbic system is the emotional center of the brain.

The amygdala, the central component of the limbic system, has roles in speech, face recognition, and translating facial expressions. It also is a short-circuit alarm system. The amygdala tells you. "Hey! Jump back!" before your intellect—the prefrontal cortex—reminds you it's a stick on the path, not a snake.

The cingulate gyrus coordinates sensory input with emotions and regulates aggressive behavior. And the hippocampus stores memories.

The brain and body are cohorts in emotional reactions. When you change body patterns, says Feldenkrais practitioner Carrie Lafferty, you change emotional patterns as well. This is especially true in the face. Dr. Ekman made faces while studying how individual muscles formed expressions. He found that angry grimaces brought the same bodily response as normal anger did: increased pulse rate, blood pressure, and body tension. A little smile may not make you happy that it's raining, though it could change your relationship to the weather.

Even botox may change emotions. An anxious woman didn't respond well to medication. But she became more relaxed and happier when botox eliminated the perpetual crease between her eyes.

The body doesn't just reflect emotions, it also triggers them, according to the ancient arts of yoga and other practices. Science is catching on.

Emotional Triggers

My friend Rosa was a successful Web designer. She always had a positive comment to share about work, entertaining, or adventures with her husband. Over a period of months, though, she became cranky, tense, and touchy. Her husband irritated her, her job was boring, and dinner parties were too much work.

Therapy, job hunt, exercise—nothing helped. Then her doctor uncovered low levels of thyroid in her blood test. Rosa found that as her thyroid came back to normal, her husband became sweeter, her job more satisfying, and cooking a delight.

Rosa's husband and boss didn't change at all—her emotions transformed as her hormones were balanced.

Emotions can occur because of what happens to you, but changes in the body, conscious thoughts, unconscious beliefs, attitudes, even your environment affect feelings.

Physical

- Hormones: Adolescence, menstrual cycles, thyroid, pregnancy, menopause, (possibly male menopause), and steroids for illness
- Facial expression, tension, and body posture
- Head injury
- Energy flow: Blockages in certain acupressure meridians, according to Chinese medicine
- Addictions
- Food: Reactions to sugar, caffeine, and not getting enough nutrients or water
- Medication
- Illness: Inward focus and pain

Mental

- Beliefs
- Self-talk and attitude (for example, optimism or pessimism)
- Images of the future

- Comparisons to others
- Expectations
- Memory
- Decision and information overload

Environmental

- Toxins
- Community: Loneliness or people-overdose
- Urban overload
- Weather (seasonal affective disorder)
- Mirror neurons: Reflecting emotions and behavior around us

Eliminating triggers can help smooth some emotions. However, no matter how many triggers you remove, life has its bumps. If your emotions are taking you for a ride—you're overwhelmed, repressed, or harm yourself or others, it's time to create some new emotional roads.

The following boosters are all different paths to the same location: having emotions without letting emotions have you. They cover thoughts, body sensations, and actions. They come from months of research as well as decades of experience in meditation, yoga, energy psychology, Feldenkrais, Restful Insomnia (a program designed to renew during sleepless nights), and Paradox Management (a system of practical spirituality).

A Caution

Emotions can be volatile for some, so as you choose a new path, go slowly and monitor your comfort and reactions. While these suggestions work for many people, be sure you have support as needed. (It doesn't hurt!) A therapist can help you determine how these boosters may work for you or suggest other paths.

☆ Emotional Boosters: Thoughts ☆

Thoughts can ignite feelings—and may change them as well. Some individuals combine focus on body, actions, and thoughts to transform their relationship to emotions.

Inner Talk

Marianne, who ranted at her family, first rants at herself. "I'm a horrible parent, the kids are lazy, and it will never get better." Changing her inner talk can change her emotions:

- **Listen.** Marianne's self-talk has negative labels (*lazy*), absolutes (*never*), predicts catastrophes about the future, and self-identifies as a bad parent.

- **Rephrase.** Marianne can rephrase her inner dialogue by focusing on her own reactions and actions: "I feel overwhelmed with piles of stuff." "I want help in cleaning." "I want to teach the kids to be more responsible." Rephrasing creates movement and responsibility because it has to do with changing oneself versus changing others.

- **Reframe.** When you look at a problem in a new light, you change your relationship to it. Identify how this struggle can support your inner growth. "I'm learning how to communicate what I want, which is useful in my whole life."

Self-Critic

If your negative self-talk is on automated replay, it generates shame, questioning, and fear—even rage, control, and addictions. There's not much room for the real you to shine. As Monk Matthieu Ricard said, you can cover gold with mud, but that "does not change the nature of gold itself." (You're the gold, by the way.)

We all have a critic, but when it strangles the lovely inner self, it's time for action. You can change your relationship to the self-critic even if you can't eliminate it.

- Rick Carson, author of *Taming Your Gremlin,* recommends that you **draw silly pictures of your critic.** He also suggests you notice the sensations on your skin, so you focus on the reality of your body rather than the convoluted lies your gremlin tells.

- **Push your self-critic outside of your body.** Use your hands and imagine it next to you, not inside. Your critic differs from your real self. Perhaps it has negative thoughts, tension, fear, and blame. And your real self (the gold) may have supportive thoughts, balance, and responsibility.

- **Talk back** to your self-critic. Not as an argument—critics don't like to give up. Instead, state the reality you want. The self-critic says, "You're stupid." You reply, "There are things I know and am learning about. I'm not going to listen to your lies."

Some people don't hear the critical voice, they just feel bad inside. That may be the sense of shame, "a painful belief in one's basic defectiveness as a human being," according to the authors of *Letting Go of Shame.* The physical experience of shame tells you when your self-critic is going haywire. It's a good reminder to check your self-talk for unseen critical grenades.

Blame is a mind-trap for emotions, especially anger. Marianne applied plenty of blame, ranting about her lazy kids. It's easy to think others will make you happy, but it's more useful to look at changing yourself.

- Is your statement physically true, or is it a belief in your head? Marianne admitted, "Well, my kids don't wash the dishes unless I nag. But they do take the trash out and wash their clothes."

- How do you react to having that blaming feeling? "I feel tense, hopeless, and angry."

- What would your life be like if you didn't have that blame? "I'd be more focused on me, instead of them. I'd like that."

- How do the words of your blame apply to you? "I'm not lazy! But . . . I might be lazy about disciplining my kids. I don't really want to create a worksheet and consequences. I just want them to do the work."

Marianne turned her blame around. Then she focused on how to be a better parent, instead of wanting her kids to fix her feelings.

Inquiry

Befriend your emotions to find new ways to relate them. Start by relaxing the body, noticing sensations, and letting answers to these questions arise.

- What am I feeling?
- What am I thinking?
- What did I just do?
- Are there similar times I've felt this?
- Are there similar triggers to this feeling, such as words or body motions?

- What happens if I intensify or minimize the sensations?

☆ Emotional Boosters: Body and Sensations ☆

With intense emotions, it's not just thoughts that drive you crazy, it's the body. Who wants a nauseous stomach, furrowed brow, and rapid heartbeats? The impulse is to get rid of what bothers you, not feel it more.

However, feelings don't last forever, especially when you experience them, learn what lessons they offer, and create a new relationship with them. A soothing anchor helps you make friends with your emotions. Your breath, body awareness, and/or energy psychology (touching places on the skin to shift emotions) are quite helpful, as are therapists and support groups.

Sit with Emotions

Here are the steps meditation teacher Sally Kempton offers as a means for expanding and understanding emotions anchored by body awareness.

1. **Acknowledge the feeling.** Name the emotion that rocks you. "I feel angry, jealous, upset."
2. **Pause.** Focus on your breath as it goes in and out. That stops the urge for action, giving you time to explore the feelings.

3. **Get grounded.** "When we're experiencing strong emotions," says Kempton, "we often lose touch with our physical body." Get grounded by noticing where you touch the earth: your feet on the floor, buttocks on a chair, back on a mattress.

4. **Become aware of your heart** and the area around it. Use your breath—as if you're breathing in and out of the heart—and your attention to highlight this "anchor space."

5. **Explore the emotional feeling.** Notice the sensation of emotion in your body. Where is it located? Is it hot or cold? Prickly or swampy? Does it have a color field? What about a sound? Does it remind you of an image . . . a fire, cage, bubbles? It may change or move. Let go any thoughts associated with this feeling for now . . . nothing to do, just be with the sensation.

6. **Hold the feeling in the heart.** Let the heart-space gently expand until it surrounds the emotional feeling. Notice how the grief or anger shifts. It may become sharper for a while or it may soften, blending and fading.

Stay with this sense of cradling your feelings. Emotions may shift from anger to sadness to understanding as you shift to a new perspective.

Express Yourself

If your emotions are telling your body to move, let it . . . with awareness and without making someone else the target.

Studies show that individuals who try to keep emotions in check stress their health. A good cry is better than feeling stalked by sadness. Discussions abound whether expressing anger increases or releases it? From my perspective, expressing *anger* releases emotional tension from your body. However, expressing *blame* fans the flames of faulting someone else.

Even Darwin knew that expressing emotions is good for the brain. "Passivity in grief," he said "loses the best chance of recovering the elasticity of the mind."

- For **anger,** pound pillows in a private place. Take a brisk walk, swing your fists, and say, "NO!" Some individuals like to yell into a pillow (but it gives me a sore throat). Knead some clay or bread dough. Write a letter you never send. Pulverize weeds in your garden.

- For **grief,** breathe into and out of your sad sensations—they may turn into tears of release. See a tearjerker movie—the *Washington Post* suggests the *Field of Dreams, E.T., Ghost.* Read a sad kids' book (*Charlotte's Web* and *Bridge to Terabithia* are good). Cuddle up to a stuffed animal or pillow, pull a blanket up, and take time to feel the loss.

However, expressing the cycle of panic may make it worse, since fearful behavior tends to keep people on guard. Keep reading for techniques to work with fear.

Tone Down Fear

Fear has a life of its own. The reaction to a fearful experience or thought (eyes wide, breath held, hypersensitivity) leads to the belief that there's something to worry about. While there *could* be something to worry about—an erratic car or an abusive partner—if might just be your own fearful images. (The book *The Gift of Fear* is useful for sorting out fear in relationships.)

- **Notice facts,** not feelings. Where are you sitting? What's happening right now?

- **Change your self-talk and images.** If you focus on problems, imagine solutions. Tone down the catastrophe from a trauma to an inconvenience. Envision the change you'll handle, not the worst.

- **Rewind** the fearful movie you project in your mind, just like you were at the cinema, suggests Ragini Michaels, Neurolinguistic Programming trainer. Imagine your inner scary movie going super-fast in reverse, with backward voices and the whoosh of the projector. When it's all reversed, imagine the global sign for NO (a red circle and slash) across the screen.

- **Say** to yourself, "I'm imagining one possible future. Not the only one."

- **Imagine a new movie** of the future you want. Feel yourself in it with sensations in your body.

- **Be grateful** for all you have.

☆ Emotional Boosters: Actions ☆

You're wired to react to emotions. Sometimes that is useful. Other times—when you want to give a rude hand gesture on the freeway—it gets you in trouble. In the heat of the moment, it may be hard to change your ingrained response. That's what renowned couples' therapists Dr. John and Julie Gottman call emotional "flooding." It puts a standstill to effective arguments, because couples can't think until they've calmed down.

Try these methods to help change your short- and long-term response to emotions.

Let the Intensity Fade

Emotional intensity fades if you're not pumping the same intense thoughts in your brain.

- **Take a time out.** It could be a few minutes or hours.
- **Get distracted.**
- **Move.** It changes emotional body patterns.

Support the Body

The intensity of emotions may fade as your basic body needs are met. Drink some water, have something nutritious when you're hungry, take a 20-minute snooze or 20-minute walk outside, take some fish oil. Exercise. Move into a heart-expanding posture. Sleep or relax at night.

Energy Psychology

Energy Psychology, detailed in chapter 2, is a category of various techniques that use touch, Eastern healing, and body-focused movements to transform the hold of emotions. Examples are EFT (Emotional Freedom Technique), TFT (Thought Field Therapy), and TAT (Tapas Acupressure Technique). Try them out. They may seem odd at first but they can really help.

Exercise:

You've probably heard that exercise helps emotion. Do you know why? Exercise:

- Detoxifies your fight-or-flight stress response
- Increases your endorphins—those natural feel-good hormones
- Acts as an outlet for anger and hostility
- Enhances your sense of personal strength and ability
- Provides time for solitude or for a social connection
- Deepens your breathing

Row, square dance, jump rope, swim, tango, fence roller blade. Stretching and yoga release emotions from a tense body.

Art and Creativity

You can ease the heartbreak of a bad relationship through art. A friend made a bright red collage with torn pictures, deceitful letters, and graffiti across it. Not beautiful, but it released the rage. Art helps cancer patients and grief groups heal. Creativity engages the brain and changes the relationship to intense emotion. Brain activity measured after painting and drawing, according to a study at Hines Veterans Hospital in Illinois, was statistically different than activity measured at a resting state. Play with creative emotional expression.

- Write a poem or a song.
- Pull out some pencils, paints, clay, and doodle, sketch, and mold. Let your body lead the way.
- Make a sand castle or snow sculpture of a guillotine.

The Opposite Emotion

Stretch your feelings; try on the opposite emotion. If you're jealous of your friend's art show, remember how much you like her sense of humor. You'll balance the spiral of resentment in others and yourself.

Breathe

People huff and puff when they're angry, or hold their breath when scared. In fact, most people regularly hold residual air in their lungs.

Before you "take a deep breath," release. Start with a l-o-n-g outbreath, say 5 seconds. Exhale the air from your tiny bronchioles on the edges of your lungs . . . could be the air you inhaled when your computer froze this morning. The next inhale just arises, deep and natural.

Music

Change your mood with songs and music. Dancing releases tension, singing helps you breathe, and the rhythm of music changes your heart beat. Familiar tunes remind you of good times. Sad songs are great for a cry—try Emmy Lou Harris or John Mayer.

Laughter

Laughter helps you breathe. It dissolves tension, stress, anxiety, anger, grief, and depression. Laughter boosts your immune system, reduces pain by releasing endorphins, and integrates both hemispheres of your brain. It's the shock absorber for life. (See chapter 2 for more on laughter.)

Read some Dave Barry, surf joke Web sites, or pretend to laugh. Could be contagious.

Emotional Learning

Emotions become great teachers, once you accept and watch them. You learn who you are, how you make choices, what triggers loneliness, which friends feel right to spend time with. According to Dr. Ekman, emotional awareness teaches you to be

1. Aware of your emotions when they begin, so you can make different choices about them
2. More sensitive to subtle signs of emotions in others, and
3. More able to communicate effectively

Emotional learning stretches the brain, even if there's no SAT test for your emotional intelligence. By befriending your emotions, you'll affect your ability to think, plan, and be present to the moment.

5

The Big Wide World and Your Brain

A true friend is someone who thinks that you are a good egg even though he knows that you are slightly cracked.

—Bernard Meltzer

Andy owns a house on 20 acres. It's environmentally green—straw-bale walls, natural latex futon, and bamboo floors. He breathes deep and happy when he drives up (in an hybrid car, of course) for weekends and vacations.

Could he live out there? Maybe. While he could work via the Internet, he'd be lonely for friends, family, grandkids. Still when they visit—with smelly plastic air mattresses, noisy toys, and tons of clutter—it's like he's back in the stressful city. He gets cranky, can't think, and spaces out.

Andy knows how his brain works best: nature, quiet, and other people. But sometimes he can't have both quiet and people at the same time.

Everyone's brain needs a supportive environment. While ideal atmosphere may not be a straw-bale house, you can create surroundings that enhance the brain. This chapter shows how to enhance your outside environment, personal space, and connections with others.

Let's start with what hurts the brain.

Neurotoxicity

Pete and Elizabeth were thrilled to pick out new carpet for their living room. It was a soothing pattern that didn't show dirt their three children brought in. But the day after the carpet was installed, their preschooler daughter started shaking and having seizures.

The chemicals in the carpet, underpad, and glue were hurting her brain.

Many people have difficulty with chemicals in carpets, plastics, and everyday products. While bodies have some defenses against toxins, the barriers in the digestive system, immune response, and even a blood-brain barrier are permeable, and toxins can get in. This can affect body organs, including the brain.

When toxins disrupt or kill neurons, it's called *neurotoxicity.* Problems arise with emotions, mental function, nervous system, behavior, and illnesses. Or so people say.

Tracking and documenting the neurotoxicity problem is controversial. It can involve many variables, says Dr. James Dahlgren, who evaluates and treats patients with exposure to toxic chemicals. Reactions to toxins can depend on how long someone was exposed, the person's age, the levels of chemicals, and combined (synergistic) effects if several chemicals were involved. Reactions may not be apparent right away, which increases the controversy about whether the symptoms are caused by chemicals. "The big wildcard," he says "is that when someone is exposed to many chemicals at the same time, no one knows what dose levels trigger brain problems."

Experts in the field say toxins can affect all areas: mental problems (memory, thinking, concentration, language, attention deficit disorder (ADD), autism, and reaction time), physical problems (sleeping, fatigue, headache, sexual dysfunction, developmental delays, numb hands and feet), emotional issues (depression, confusion, personality changes), behavior (irrational, criminal, or violent behavior), and overall illnesses (movement disorders, multiple sclerosis, chemical sensitivity).

No life is perfectly healthy—last I checked, we all die. Still, we can make our lives safer, to minimize exposure and possible long-term effects of toxins.

Toxins

While some individuals are more sensitive to chemicals, all of us can take action. This section lists some common problems and recommendations that can keep our brains less toxic.

We live in a sea of **plastics**—cheap, unbreakable, and flexible. While plastics have advanced the medical field, they're not without dangers to bodies and the Earth. Smelly plastics, like new shower curtains, are most likely made from PVCs (polyvinyl chlorides). PVC plastics use chlorine as well as heavy metals and other toxic plasticizers to soften or stabilize the material. Dioxins are produced during manufacture and incineration of plastics. Not good, since dioxins are the most potent animal carcinogen ever tested and cause of a host of other problems, according to the Natural Resources Defense Council.

Avoid plastics made from PVCs that say "vinyl" in the product name or have the number 3 recycling code, and replace with products made from other types of plastic. While they may cost more, they increase your health and safety. Here are some ideas:

Start with eliminating PVCs from toys, which include a highly toxic material called *phthalates* to soften the plastic.

Polyester liners are a good substitute for shower curtains. Most food wrap and bags have been made from polyethylene instead of PVC since 2005, says Ziploc customer service. And that new car smell? It's not the smell of money. It's chemicals from plastic. For more information, check the Vinyl Exam article at the Washington Toxics Coalition Web site (*www.watoxics.org/homes-and-gardens/factsheets/vinyl*).

Those toxic phthalates in toys also end up in **cosmetics**—which may also contain mercury, lead, and untested nanoparticles. *Nanoparticles* are tiny ingredients that may be able slide up the optic nerve to the brain, according to Sally Tinkle, a researcher at the National Institute of Environmental Health Sciences. The Environmental Working Group has a cosmetics database that lists both harmful and safer cosmetics (*www.cosmeticsdatabase.com*).

Keep your garden and home (and brain and body) healthy by minimizing or **eliminating herbicides and pesticides.** For instance, make a solution of nontoxic boric acid and sugar on cotton balls to naturally eliminate tiny ants from your home. Your state extension office (at *http://www.csrees.usda.gov/Extension*) has regional information about good alternatives to herbicides and pesticides. Yard chemicals can easily travel in the house via shoes and clothing to get onto our bodies, or those of kids who spend much time on the floor. Taking shoes off at the door can lessen outdoor toxins inside.

Would you feed your baby **flame retardants**? Human breast milk in the United States has the highest levels of polybrominated diphenyl ether (PBDE) in the world: 10 to 20 times higher than those in Europe, according to the Environmental Working Group. Studies in mice and rats show that flame retardants may cause cognitive and behavior problems and increase cancer rates.

Flame retardants are found in many seat cushions, carpet padding, TV and computer wire insulation, mattress stuffing, and Styrofoam. These chemicals are slow to degrade and are found in dust particles. What can you do? Buy PBDE-free furniture (IKEA is one source) and reduce use of foam. Substitute wool padding and covers for furniture, says the Green Guide. Check out *http://www.pollutioninpeople.org* for other safe furniture choices. Choose electronics from companies that have eliminated PBDEs and toxic chemicals. Find a list at *http://www.watoxics.org/issues/pbde/pbde-resources* or contact the companies directly.

What can be dangerous about **wood**? It can have chemicals that get into your brain when it off-gasses or you breathe dust from working with it. Formaldehyde is in particle board, arsenic in preservatives, and copper chromium arsenate in treated wood (wood with little lines all over it). Since chemicals in treated wood can come off on hands and the ground, don't use it for playground equipment, on deck surfaces, or as borders in a food garden, says David Stizhal, of Full Circle Environmental consulting firm. The Washington Toxic Coalition Web site has healthier alternatives: *www.watoxics.org/homes-and-gardens/resources-treated-wood*.

Carbon monoxide can lead to brain damage and death. You can't see or smell carbon monoxide, and low levels of poisoning may give you flu-like symptoms. The chemical compound is created by incomplete burning in gas hot water heaters and furnaces, fireplaces, wood stoves, and car exhaust. You can get a carbon monoxide detector for your home and have your chimney checked. While driving, make sure your muffler is healthy, don't run your car in a garage, and avoid trailing smelly cars and trucks—or recirculate the air vent when you have to follow them.

Complaints about **new carpets** are common, ranging from rashes, fatigue, runny nose, burning sensation in the eyes, headaches, and even seizures. Off-gassing chemicals come from synthetic fibers, glue, dyes, fire and moth proofing, and stain resistors. Green-label carpets reduce some of those chemicals. The U.S. Consumer Product Safety Commission (CPSC) suggests that you

- Ask the retailer to unroll and air out the carpet in a well-ventilated area before installation
- Use low-emitting adhesives
- Ventilate the newly carpeted room
- Leave the house during installation and for several hours afterward (though some allergists suggest it may take a few days or weeks to out-gas)

Heavy Metals

I knew someone who had five old root canals redone to eliminate mercury in the fillings. And I know wonderful dentists who roll their eyes at the mercury hysteria. Controversy rages over whether heavy metals promote diseases such as fibromyalgia, multiple sclerosis, lupus, and autism. On the one hand, the amount of mercury absorbed by amalgam fillings and vaccines is below the official level for adverse health effects. On the other hand, there's concern that any mercury, especially so near the brain, is detrimental.

Still, it is important to protect fetal brains from heavy metal, says Dr. James Dahlgren. Women wanting to get pregnant should get their blood levels checked for heavy metals. Check with resources on both sides of the argument to protect your wallet and your physical and mental health.

- **Minimize mercury** contact by bringing used mercury instruments (like your old home thermostat or compact fluorescent bulbs) to a proper recycler. Ask manufacturers to stop using mercury or to take their products back for disposal.
- Eat **fish,** but not those with too much mercury and other metals. Oceans Alive (*www.oceansalive.org*) has an easy-to-use list of safe fish to eat.
- Older homes, mostly from before 1960, may have lead in the oil-based **paint.** Dust and paint chips are

detrimental, especially for children. The Consumer Product Safety Commission suggests you remove or repaint the lead-painted areas or at least damp-mop to remove lead dust.

- **Drinking water** may contain lead from pollution or plumbing pipes in the home or the water system. If a test shows lead, filter your water, and check with a plumber or municipality to determine the source. Filtering also removes chlorine, microorganisms, and synthetic chemicals in the water supply from pesticides, herbicides, dry cleaning, and other sources.
- Whether **aluminum** causes Alzheimer's disease has not been proven, according to the Alzheimer's Society. However those who want to reduce aluminum should monitor levels in water, antiperspirants, and aluminum cookware. Aluminum foil, they say, leaves a negligible amount of aluminum in food.

What to Do

Use your body to monitor your environment and health. Rashes, headaches, or flu symptoms may have an environmental trigger—especially if there's new carpet, cabinets, or paint. Your sense of smell can steer you from other dangerous products: paint, mothballs, stain and paint thinners, a stinky lawn mower.

Keep informed about chemicals. However, be careful where your information comes from. According to Dr. Dahlgren, industries have had influence on scientific research that has corrupted many reports. Check for the bias or industry funding of the author or researchers.

Take action in your community and political system to encourage laws that regulate toxic materials—or support an organization that does so.

Find balance. You can control some toxins in your life. And you can control stress by enjoying life, which provides a happier brain. Toast your dinner of healthy fish with a glass (not plastic cup) of filtered water, and give thanks.

Over-Over-Overload?

Pop-up ads, cell phone calls, traffic noise, time crunch, clutter . . . we're in overload. We live in "Attention Economy," flooded with stimulation.

Chaos means distraction, said Dr. Joan Borysenko, author of *Minding the Body, Mending the Mind.* "It's not that I can't write when the office is a mess," she told me, "but a clean office sharpens the ax." Mess suppresses the brain's activity and ability to respond, reported Dr. Robert Desimone in research at the National Institute of Mental Health. A cluttered scene suppresses activity in a critical circuit for recognizing objects. Too much stimulation, he said, requires too much attention.

Reduce Clutter

Marla Cilley, the FlyLady from her book *Sink Reflections* and Web site *www.flylady.com*, says clutter consists of things you aren't sure you really want—a pile of unmade decisions. Small clutter-reducing steps make a big difference.

- **TMS** is what my husband calls "Too Much Stuff." Find twenty things that have no value (broken, unusable, expired, or unwanted). Throw them out, recycle, or give them away. If you do this once a week—even once a month—your home gets miraculously larger.
- **Clean** a spot or a room: Use a timer and clean for 15 minutes a day until it's done. This clean spot becomes a haven when you're overloaded.
- Buy **less stuff.** Good for your wallet, the Earth, and your brain has fewer decisions to make.
- **Give things away.** Altruism triggers the pleasure center in the primitive brain and looks good in the house. Put a few items in the give-away box and see how it feels. Or take pictures and have a photo album of memories.
- **Hire a professional organizer** to arrange your papers, holiday decorations, clothes, basement, garage, and any other chaos running your brain. Check out referrals from friends or the National Association of Professional Organizers at *http://www.napo.net*.

- **Use overstimulation.** Romance author Jill Barnett told me she likes writing in crowded coffee shops. She focuses over the distracting noise and movement. May not work as well at home, with your own ringing telephone.

☆ Boosters: Time ☆

When you multitask or task-switch, you get less done and tax your brain. Multitasking adds errors and slows reaction time—it can double the time to complete tasks rather than doing them one at a time, according to the Brain, Cognition and Action Laboratory at the University of Michigan. It affects your workday. On average, employees switch tasks every 3 minutes, get interrupted every 2 minutes, and have a "long-term" stretch of twelve minutes, says Gloria Mark, professor at University of California-Irvine.

The brain gets confused, can't focus, and takes shortcuts during multitasking. Take your brain and life back:

- **Reduce information overload.** Recycle junk mail or get on the Direct Marketing Association's Mail Preference Service at *http://www.the-dma.org/consumers/offmailinglist.html*. Eliminate junk telephone calls at *http://www.donotcall.gov*. Use a spam filter to cut down on the email junk.

- **Say "No."** If you did all the great things that only require "10 minutes a day," you wouldn't have time for sleep. Balance the need for taking care of others and taking care of yourself by saying, "Sorry, I can't." No excuse or explanation required.

- **Limit television.** Your brain doesn't recharge while you watch. Research shows that when you watch television, higher brain regions (the neocortex and midbrain, for example) shut down, and activity shifts to the reactive lower "reptile" brain. TV may also numb the left hemisphere, which handles organization, analysis, and judgment of incoming data. And to add icing to the cake, only 30 seconds of television causes a semi-comatose, hypnotic brain. Instead of watching to see the next loser in "American Idol," turn it off. Hide it. Put it in an inconvenient spot. Trade down for a 19-inch model. Cancel cable. Eliminate one regular show. Eliminate a day a week. Once you're weaned from one-way TV friends, your brain will find lots to enjoy.

- **Get off the computer.** Computers offer a maze of distractions that can cause insomnia and addiction. Insomnia is triggered by increased light, stimulation, and emotional intensity, especially for those playing computer games, say Japanese researchers. Those addicted to computers may have difficultly limiting their use and actually feel euphoric on the computer, says Harvard professor Dr. Maressa Orzack, founder of Computer Addiction Services. Help yourself by creating computer limits. An automatic calendar notation reminds you to turn off the computer in the evening, so you go to bed. When you work on other projects, close the Internet and even email. Create a weekly noncomputer day. Install parental control software—ask a friend to install your own settings.

- Excuse me, I have to answer my **cell phone.** Take your power back by choosing when to have it on, and use voicemail. Unplug and live.

☆ Boosters: Lights and Noise ☆

It's hard to avoid invasive lights and noise. However, you may be able to reduce the amounts and your reactions.

- If the **noise is ongoing,** insulate the walls or hang some soundproof material on walls, doors, or ceiling. Get double-paned glass windows. Mask sounds with white noise (machines or fans) that reduces the contrast between the noise and quiet. Play a CD of the beach, a waterfall, or even a clothes dryer or vacuum (really!). Get some sound-reducing earphones. Or try earplugs, in silicone, foam, or discontinued models made from down and foam.

- Is your **attitude creating the noise problem**? One person might be bothered by a barking dog, and another might enjoy it—the sound of life. Spend some moments listening to noise and silence, rather than judging whether they're okay.

- You need **light during the day:** natural light from that nearby star, the sun. During winter, you may get cranky and sleepy from darkness—seasonal affective disorder. There's also an increase in diseases such as multiple sclerosis in darker climes, according to the Multiple Sclerosis Center of the University of San Francisco. Get outside, especially in the morning. Try a light box or light alarm in winter. Take your vitamin D.

- The brain and body need **darkness** to rest. The pineal gland in the brain produces the relaxing hormone melatonin at dusk—if you have dusk! Instead we have city street lights, TV, computers, and lights in every room. A few hours before bed, turn off lights and use softer lamps. Install room-darkening blinds or curtains. Change outside lights to motion detectors. Use a comforting eye mask to relax into the dark.

Beauty and the Brain

What does beauty have to do with brain power? For Dr. Joan Borysenko, "Beauty allows me to focus." She configures her desk so she sees a beautiful plant or painting when she turns. She plays beautiful harp music to evoke a mood, or she enjoys the silence. She determines what she needs before she begins a task, asking herself, "What would be concentrating, energizing, inspiring, relaxing?" Reducing stimulation reveals the soothing power of beauty in the brain.

Reducing stimulation reveals the soothing power of beauty in the brain.

Your own idea of beauty may be enhanced through ancient traditions like feng shui, color therapists, and other ideas:

- Amber hues beat fatigue. Green is evocative of nature. Yellow energizes. Blue calms. At least that's the expert opinion of **color therapists.** How do you respond to colors? Paint a new color on the wall, hang pictures, drape scarves or curtains. See what you like. Keep color changes simple at first, so you can distinguish the colors that shine for you.
- Asian traditions such as **feng shui** say that your house or work environment has energy rivers—

meridians—just like your body does. How you arrange your furniture in your house affects how that energy flows for happiness, wealth, and health.

- **Music** not only creates a mood, it also calms, motivates, and helps you heal. Does Mozart help you think better? That's controversial, though the beauty of music is ingrained in the brain. "All humans come into the world with an innate capability for music," says Kay Shelemay, professor of music at Harvard. According to research on the brain reviewed in the *Harvard Gazette,* babies squirm at dissonant music at four months and coo for tunes they like. When heart bypass patients heard background music in recovery from surgery, they needed lower doses of blood pressure medicine. Music played in the neonatal intensive care, along with humming from mothers and nurses, helped premature babies gain weight faster and leave the units earlier. Music calms Alzheimer's patients and can help stroke victims relearn language. Dance music gets you moving. A little night music can help relax the body. Try music without words when you're working and keep a repertoire of music to enhance your life.

- **Plants and nature** sustain the brain. In 1984, Harvard biologist Dr. Edward Wilson called the natural love of nature *biophilia.* This natural connection helps speed healing. Researchers found that watching nature—be it an aquarium or hedge—lowered blood pressure and increased relaxation. A window to the outside world, even a picture of nature, shortened hospital stays. It's easy to bring a little natural beauty into your life. Art or photographs of landscapes can relax the eyes. Plants provide oxygen and moisture to indoor air and reduce dust. Indoor plants can lessen fatigue, coughs, and sore throats by more than 30 percent, according to Norwegian researchers. NASA Space Research found that ordinary spider plants and peace lilies effectively cleaned the air. That may help with some of those toxins mentioned earlier.

- **Bring in the light.** Natural sunlight from windows or skylights provides light that's relaxing and energizing. By contrast, fluorescents can flicker with a greenish cast; regular incandescent bulbs have a yellow tint; halogens can produce glare. Full-spectrum lights, according to their manufacturers, stimulate the rods and cones in your eyes, although the sun provides the best full spectrum available.

You can appreciate beauty in a whole new way when you share it with a community of family and friends. *That* stimulates your brain.

Community

My friend Christopher wished he wasn't a smoker. He tried to quit again and again. But when he was stressed or wanted to hang out with smoking friends, he borrowed one or two cigarettes. Then he bought a pack and was back at it.

He finally quit his Marlboros, and it wasn't nicotine gum that did the trick. Instead it was the support system he created: friends, coworkers, even the smokers outside. They helped him restructure his habits as he reinvented himself into a non-smoker. By using his social brain, Christopher changed his thoughts, emotions, and smoking habit.

"Social behavior is a brain function just like memory or language," says Dr. John Ratey in *User's Guide to the Brain.* The social brain helps individuals and the clan of humans survive.

Social functions energize the whole brain. You remember faces and names, talk about politics, move your body, have feelings, think about what you hear, watch what you eat—all at the same time. "Our highest human virtue is our connection with other humans, and social activity is basic to our health and happiness," says Dr. Ratey.

When you engage in social functions, your brain works better. Married men live an average of ten years longer than nonmarried men, according to the Population Research Association of America. Those over the age of seventy who had strong friendships were more likely (by 22 percent) to live more than ten years longer than those who didn't, according the Australian Longitudinal Study of Aging.

A rich social network may decrease the risk of developing dementia, according to Swedish research, because it increases social interaction and intellectual stimulation. And the National Institute of Mental Health says that participating in religious, social, or other activities can help depression.

No matter whether you're shy, lost friends due to relocation or deaths, or are clueless about social interactions and small talk, you can still maximize your social brain.

☆ Boosters: Increase Your Connections ☆

Temple Grandin, the autistic author of *Unwritten Rules of Social Relationships,* didn't know how to approach people. Either she pounced on them or hung back in the distance.

While her social skills were lacking, her logical mind helped her learn about social contact. Temple walked through automatic doors at grocery stores—over and over again—to find the right speed to approach people. She found other ways to learn people skills, and she wrote "rules" that help everyone: focus on diplomacy (versus honesty) and politeness, understand that everyone makes social mistakes, and monitor whether you turn people off.

As with any skill, connecting with new people takes practice. Here are some ways to increase or engage with those around you.

Activities

- Take **classes** at adult education centers, community colleges, art schools, tai chi or yoga centers, community centers, and more. You can meet others during the class or an after-class coffee while you're learning a new skill.

- **Hobbies** provide community through classes, clubs, associations, and mini-conventions. Even knitters have community, such as "Stitch and Pitch" nights when fans bring their needles and yarn to a baseball game.

- **Eating with others** is a social as well as survival endeavor. Set up regular monthly lunches with friends or social group. Have potlucks or dinner parties, or arrange an ongoing restaurant tour of your favorite ethnic cuisine.

- Create a **book group** with friends or find ones at a community college, religious organization, or library.

- **Game nights.** Some taverns have trivia nights, bookstores may have chess or board game nights, or you can invite friends to play Cranium, Pictionary, or Apples to Apples. Games make you laugh and ease small talk.

- Join an **association** for businesses, hobbies, and interests. Many meetings of the Chamber of Commerce or small business owners offer introductory breakfasts or luncheons. Toastmasters develop self-confidence in public speaking and connect you to others, in meetings and speeches.

- Check out your **online newspaper or Craigslist** for events, meetings, and people looking to connect. When I scanned the "activity partner" section of the Boston Craigslist I found ads for soccer players, foreign language buddies, hiking partners, poker players, Ikea shoppers, classical music companions, and dragon boat racers.

Inner needs:

- **Volunteer** to meet others . . . and become happier as well. Volunteer work counters negative moods such as depression and anxiety and makes life more satisfying, say researchers at the University of Texas-Austin and the University of Zurich. In addition, altruism is hard-wired to be pleasurable, activating a part of the brain that usually lights up in response to food or sex. Volunteer coordinators at nonprofits or the United Way can guide you to donate your skills in business, child care, administration, music, and pet care. And you can learn new skills as well.

- Connect to others at **religious or spiritual organizations.** "People who are involved in faith have a support group to call on" to help them to move through the down times, says Dr. Todd Clements. Connect with others before or after services, in a class, or volunteer to help with an event.

- **Twelve-step meetings** and other groups at health organizations can provide a network of people who support you through illness, grief, or changing addictive behaviors. Try a few different meetings to find one that's a good match.

Other Connections:

- Take Fido to the **dog park,** a nursing home, dog training, or a regular dog-populated area. Say hello to other dogs—and owners. You might find groups for ferret and parrot owners at pet stores. Good luck with cat groups, though.

- Connect to others through **touch and movement.** Try dancing classes or events (folkdance, ballroom, contra, jazz, or square dances). Take a class in foot reflexology or massage.

Your Environmental Brain

There's no perfect place to live, since everything changes. But, like Andy, you can clean up your living space, create beauty for yourself, and connect with others. Even if you can't do it all at once.

Your brain is here to interact with the big wide world—so appreciate the big wide world you interact with.

6

Eating for Brilliance

Red meat is not bad for you. Now blue-green meat,
that's bad for you!

—Tommy Smothers

The evening news announced research on the food you ate for lunch: it destroys your knee caps, creates toxins in a sandwich, and may be healthy when combined with expensive Antarctic turnips. Or something like that.

We've been in food information overkill ever since scientists discovered that you *are* what you eat. Contradictory studies analyze every type of food, vitamin, mineral, herb, and combination thereof. Even so, research does reveal old-time wisdom: what you swallow makes you smarter and happier (or slower and more blue).

Still, all that scientific wisdom may not change our habits. We eat quickly, exciting our taste buds with fats, sugars, processed grains, artificial colors, and preservatives that keep food in stable animation forever. We're buzzed . . . then our energy plummets. We feel moody and stupid. We need a latte. Or a cure-all vitamin.

Time for the science of the body—discover foods that feed the growth of your brain. It's easy to find food, herbs, and supplements that support thinking, memory, and moods—instead of those that zap it. Keep reading this chapter full of ideas and boosters, and adjust your diet to boost your brain's brilliance.

The Brain Diet

Your brain still grows, even if you're ancient—over twenty. Scientists used to think that you were born with all the neurons you'd ever have. If you drank alcohol as an adult and killed brain cells . . . well, good luck. Then in 1998, researchers discovered the birth of new neurons in individuals who were near death. Turns out your brain—no matter how old or young—can generate new neurons, too.

One key to brain growth? Diet.

What you eat helps generate healthy neurons with bushes of dendrites (nerve receptors; see Figure 1.4). It also keeps nerve endings firing and allows you to maintain brain flexibility—*neuroplasticity.* Even if your memory's so fried you can't remember your spouse's cell phone number, food still provides brain sustenance:

- **A stable source of energy.** Your brain uses 20 percent of your energy, even though it's only 2 percent of your weight.
- **Nutrients.** Nourishing food helps your brain manufacture chemicals (*neurotransmitters*) that transmit signals to help you feel good, ignore distractions, and remember phone numbers.
- **Antioxidants** keep the brain "clean" by reducing the effect of oxidation (like rust) in cells.
- **Useful fats.** Essential fatty acids (EFA) help protect the cell membrane, transmit messages, reduce inflammation, and support reproduction of neurons.
- **Water.** The brain is 78 percent water; a thirsty brain is dull and unhappy.

What foods make the brain happy? We can survive on a huge variety of food—éclairs to eggplant—but our diet drives our thinking, moods, memory. You can bump along in an Edsel or cruise in a Rolls Royce.

You'll find an Edsel diet in boxes on the grocery shelves. You'll find a Rolls Royce diet back in time . . . during the Stone Age. The earliest humans ate what was best for the brain, says Jean Carper, author of *Your Miracle Brain:* "The essence—the biochemistry and physiology—of our brains is fine-tuned to a long-lost diet that existed in prehistoric days."

The Stone Age diet (also called the Cave Man, Paleolithic, or Evolution diet) consists of animal protein like wild game and fish; nuts, legumes, and seeds; veggies and fruits; and a little honey. They're not talking chocolate cookies or fries. Even rice, milk, and beef weren't available then.

Do you need to live in Fred Flintstone's cave (okay, it was a prehistoric Rambler) and never look pizza in the eye? No, you can still eat today's foods. The question is in what proportion. Right now, less than 45 percent of the typical American diet is Stone Age. The rest consists of foods that need cultivation or processing: cereal, grains (especially wheat and gluten-based grains), processed oils, sugar, milk products, and alcohol.

The more Stone Age foods we eat, the better we'll feel, says Carper. You don't have to go cold turkey—literally. Inch your way, meal by meal, adding veggies and fruits, reducing refined carbs, keeping lean, and eating fish or fish oils.

Here are foods that help your brain (and body, too).

Fat

Fat. A bad word. We don't want to look fat, feel fat, or eat fat—according to diets of the past decades.

But there is more than one kind of fat. Some fats wreak havoc on your brain and body. Other fats are essential for your brain. What's the difference? It's how the molecule chains in the fats are arranged and bonded.

You've got fats like **saturated fats** and **trans fats,** which lay flat and stack on each other, according to nutritionist Sharon Maffett. Saturated fats are found in milk, red meat, lard, butter, cream, processed snacks, and other grocery products. Trans fats are oils solidified with hydrogen to form processed poly- and monosaturated fat. They're found in French fries, packaged cupcakes, shortening, microwaved popcorn, crackers, and more.

Our brains do not like these fats. They disrupt nerve communication and mental performance and set the stage for cells to degenerate. And there's more! Saturated fats clog arteries, hamper glucose (energy) metabolism, increase the rate of Parkinson's disease, increase insulin resistance (prediabetic and diabetic states impair thinking and memory), increase inflammation (a precursor to Alzheimer's and other neurological diseases), and interfere with your brain's access to the useful fats.

You won't become brain-dead from an occasional fast-food cheeseburger. But if your regular rations are filled with saturated fats, you're keeping your learning and memory below par. Animals that ate a 40 percent fat diet (the standard American fare) had more dysfunction in learning, memory, and spatial perception, according to University of Toronto research. The higher the level of saturated fat they consumed, the less the animals learned.

What about other fats? **Mono-unsaturated fats** are found in avocados, nuts, and olive, peanut, and canola oils. **Polyunsaturated fats** are found in corn, sunflower, and soy oils. These are good oils, though they're not enough for brain health, since your brain only uses them if the fats it really needs aren't around.

The really good fats? **Essential fatty acids.** They're longer-chain polyunsaturated fats from coldwater fish, walnuts, flaxseed, and certain vegetable oils.

Good Fats

Your brain loves essential fatty acids, which are vital in cell functioning.

There are different kinds of EFAs (omega-3, -6, and -9), but omega-3s are the *crème de la fat* for the brain. They comprise part of cell membranes and neurons, the eye's light-sensitive retinal tissue, and the large portion of gray matter (the thinking part) of your brain.

The really good fats? Essential fatty acids. They're longer-chain polyunsaturated fats from coldwater fish, walnuts, flaxseed, and certain vegetable oils.

Studies from the past twenty-five years show how omega-3s help mood, cognition, disease prevention, and much more. While a few of the studies mentioned following are preliminary, it seems that omega-3s:

- Critically support brain and nerve development in fetuses, babies, children, teens, and adults
- Act as anti-inflammatories (chronic inflammation causes brain impairment and may lead to Alzheimer's disease)
- Reduce stress and depression, including postpartum depression, and perhaps bipolar disorder
- Reduce the chance of stroke
- Reduce risk factors for heart disease and diabetes by lowering blood pressure and cholesterol levels and triglycerides (bad cholesterol)
- Increase weight loss as part of a weight reduction program
- Assist with rheumatoid and osteoarthritis

- Increase calcium and bone density for osteoporosis
- Assist with attention deficit disorder (ADD)
- May help with eating disorders
- Help skin disorders such as photodermatitis, psoriasis, and acne; help animals recover from burns (research is on the way with humans)
- Reduce menstrual pain
- Reduce the risk of colon cancer, prostate cancer, and possibly breast cancer
- Help with asthma, inflammatory bowel syndrome, and macular degeneration in preliminary research
- Help treat ulcers, migraine headaches, preterm labor, emphysema, glaucoma, Lyme disease, lupus, and panic attacks

Even a list half as long would make you consider adding this wonder food to your diet.

Wonder *foods,* actually: there are different omega-3s. Your brain thrives on the long-chain omega-3s called EPA (eicosapentaenoic acid) and DHA (docosahexaenoic acid); they're available from fish and algae. The other omega-3 is ALA (alpha-linolenic acid) available from plants such as flax, canola, soy, English walnuts, with lesser amounts in hemp, black currant, pumpkin, and other oils or seeds. Your body can convert some ALA to the other omega-3s, but vegans should check with a nutritionist to make sure they're getting enough DHA and EPA from marine plant sources.

DHA and EPA, key fatty acids for your brain, come from wild salmon and also mackerel, halibut, scallops, sardines, herring, algae, and fish oil. Some of us remember being given cod liver oil as kids—and yes, it was good for the brain.

Is there a downside to eating fish? Pollution. Many fish are tainted with mercury and toxins, which can cause memory loss, among other debilitating disorders. Memory loss is not what we're looking for. The U.S. Department of Agriculture (USDA) and the American Stroke Association recommend you still eat two servings of fish per week from those species with less mercury toxicity. (The Seafood Watch Program from the Monterey Bay Aquarium has a good Web site: *www.mbayaq.org/cr/seafoodwatch.asp*.)

Supplements are another source of omega-3s. You can take fish oil or cod liver oil (which has additional vitamins) from companies that certify that their products are free of heavy metals such as mercury. To avoid fish oil "tuna burps," take capsules before breakfast, divide the dose among several meals, use lemon- or orange-flavored liquid cod liver oil, freeze fish oil capsules, or take them before bed. Since these oils thin the blood, tell your doctor before surgery, and individuals who are on medications like warfarin (Coumadin) or aspirin should get regular monitoring. Nutritionist Sharon Moffett recommends taking no more than 3 grams of omega-3s per day.

The U.S. Department of Agriculture (USDA) and the American Stroke Association recommend you eat two servings of fish per week from those species with less mercury toxicity.

What about the other omega oils? Your body can manufacture omega-9 if it has omega-3s. Meanwhile, omega-6 fatty acids are plentiful in a modern diet, though they have the opposite function of omega-3s: they increase blood clotting, cell proliferation, and inflammation (to clean out germs).

The recommended ratio of omega-6s to omega-3s is 5:1 to 3:1 . . . although Dr. Andrew Weil and other alternative providers suggest a 1:1 ratio. Want to guess the current American ratio? Try 20:1 to 50:1. Our processed foods and oils add up.

When you lack omega-3s, your body will choose other fats instead—leaving you grumpy, with less energy for thinking, according to research at the University of Pittsburgh and Brown University.

Your brain will be happier if you add omega-3s and reduce other fats, especially saturated and trans fats, but also mono- and polyunsaturated fats, according to Dr. Weil. Olive oil is a good alternative, as it helps keep the ratio in better balance.

Vitamins

Your brain needs vitamins to protect itself, communicate, and clean itself. The brain needs cleaning because neurons age and die—naturally or by damage from certain foods or toxins such as cigarette smoke.

When these neurons (and other body cells) oxidize and die, they create damaging free radicals—cell rust. They mutate cell membranes, alter DNA, and can cause cell death. Antioxidants in vegetables and fruits reduce, neutralize, and may prevent the damage free radicals cause.

Brains Adore Vitamins

Here are the vitamins highly touted for the brain, from sources including the University of Maryland.

B Vitamins help with energy, nerve connections, and nerve health.

- **Thiamin** metabolizes glucose, the brain's primary energy source, which synthesizes neurotransmitters. It's found in enriched grain products, pork, legumes, nuts, seeds, and organ meats.
- **Vitamin B-12** maintains the nerve cell's outer coating, which prevents nerve damage and impaired brain

function, including dementia and brain atrophy. Animal foods such as milk, meat, and eggs have B-12, as do some fortified cereals, nutritional yeast, and soymilks.

- **Folic acid or folate** is crucial for proper brain function. Folate may be the nutrient most largely associated with depression. Folate increases cognitive function and reduces the risk of Alzheimer's disease by controlling the amino acid homocysteine in the blood. Pregnant woman take folate to reduce neural tube defects in their babies. Chow down on spinach, turnip greens, Romaine lettuce, liver, brewers' yeast, asparagus, dried beans and peas, wheat, broccoli, some nuts, as well as enriched grain products.

- **Vitamin B-6** is essential to producing most of the brain's neurotransmitters. Studies show that men high in B-6 had dramatically better working memory. Along with B-12 and folate, B-6 helps you process S-adenosylmethionine (SAMe). Without SAMe, you're more likely to have depression, dementia, or a degeneration of nerves. B-6 is found in chicken, fish, pork, whole wheat products, brown rice, and some fruits and vegetables.

Vitamin C is an essential antioxidant we get from citrus fruits, parsley, bell pepper, strawberries, papaya, and crustacean veggies (broccoli, cauliflower, kale, mustard greens, and Brussels sprouts). Vitamin C helps synthesize the neurotransmitter norepinephrine and serotonin, critical to brain function and mood. Vitamin C helps transport fat for brain energy by synthesizing carnitine.

As an antioxidant, it protects proteins, fats, carbohydrates, and DNA from damage by free radicals—polluting cell exhaust. Vitamin C recycles other antioxidants, such as vitamin E, and it helps produce collagen for blood vessels.

Vitamin E is an antioxidant that readily enters the brain. It is a blood thinner. It may help prevent Alzheimer's disease, especially when taken with vitamin C. The verdict is out whether vitamin E supplementation improves cognitive function for healthy individuals and those with non-Alzheimer's dementia (for example, individuals who've had several strokes). However, excessive vitamin E may not benefit your health, as shown in recent studies. You can get vitamin E from wheat germ, vegetable oils, nuts, avocados, green leafy vegetables, and fortified cereals.

Minerals

Minerals—even trace elements—help brain health. Diet is the best source.

- **Boron** is a trace mineral with a critical role as coenzyme in chemical reactions. Boron increases cognitive ability, says the National Institutes of Health, strengthens the immune system, increases the amount of calcium that is absorbed from food, boosts energy utilization, and positively affects cholesterol production. Some reports say that boron increases memory and hand-eye coordination as well as easing menstrual symptoms, arthritis, and osteoporosis. You can get boron from fruit (pears, apples, peaches, grapes, and raisins); nuts and peanuts; leafy veggies; beans. About 1–3 mg. of boron usually comes from healthy diets, though no recommended daily allowance has been set.

- **Iron** is essential to form hemoglobin, which carries oxygen for the brain's energy process. Without enough iron, you may be slowed by anemia. Iron is best absorbed in meat, poultry, and fish and is available in whole or enriched grains, green leafy vegetables, dried beans and peas, and dried fruits.
- **Magnesium** helps transmit nerve impulses. A deficiency creates nervousness and twitching. You'll find magnesium in green leafy vegetables, firm tofu, halibut, potato skins, whole grains, nuts, seeds, bananas . . . and chocolate.
- **Manganese** is a trace mineral that contributes to brain functioning. Manganese is primarily found in whole grains and nuts.
- **Copper** deficiency impairs brain and immune system functions, changing certain chemical receptors in the

brain and lowering levels of neurotransmitters. Copper is in organ meats, seafood, nuts, seeds, whole grain breads and cereals, and chocolate (another excuse for a brownie!).

- **Zinc** maintains cell membranes and protects cells from damage. Zinc deficiency can create neurological problems, sensory impairment, and reactions from apathy and fatigue to irritability and jitteriness. Zinc is found in red meats, liver, eggs, dairy products, vegetables, and some seafood.
- **Selenium** helps synthesize some hormones and protect cell membranes from damage. It's found in seafood, liver, and eggs, and, depending on the soil, certain grains, and seeds, including Brazil nuts.

Natural Coloring

The rainbow of red tomatoes, deep green kale, amber squash, and delectable blueberries is a pot of gold: vitamins, minerals, and phytochemicals (active health-protecting and antioxidant compounds) make your brain brilliant.

Can you get your fruit and veggie quotient by pill? While some known vitamins, minerals, and even antioxidants are in supplements, phytochemicals can't be "duplicated and put into nutritional supplements," says Jennifer Thompson, a clinical dietitian with Baylor University Medical Center.

Veggies

Vegetables help your thinking. The elderly who ate nearly three servings of veggies every day slowed their natural aging cognitive decline by 40 percent, according to the Chicago Health and Aging Project. That's a chunk of smarts to keep. Even though fruits offer other benefits, in this study they didn't increase cognitive change.

Avocados are smooth, creamy packages of nutrition for the brain. Not only are they full of fiber, vitamins, and potassium, they're almost as good a blueberries for promoting brain health, says Steven Pratt, author of *Superfoods Rx: Fourteen Foods Proven to Change Your Life*. Its mono-saturated fat contributes to healthy blood flow and lower blood pressure.

Greens, such as spinach, kale, and collards, help reduce natural cognitive aging. Older rats fed lots of spinach significantly improved their learning and motor skills capacity. Spinach may lessen brain damage from strokes and disorders.

Sweet potatoes and other deeply colored veggies are full of B-6, the antioxidant vitamin C, and beta-carotene.

Cruciferous veggies (broccoli, cabbage, collard greens) have vitamins and a chemical called indole-3-carinol that repairs damaged DNA.

For some, eating veggies is like paying taxes—not at the top of the to-do list. Adult super-tasters (those with lots of taste buds) may need to blend veggies into other foods to make them more palatable. The old dietary recommendation was five servings of fruits and veggies per day. If you already munch on produce, up your servings to 9–10 a day (the USDA now suggests 5–9 a day).

Build a regular habit of eating more veggies—one extra serving a day, then add another after a few weeks. A serving is one whole vegetable, a half-cup cooked veggies, or 1 cup raw greens. They're crunchy (great when you're cranky) and good to nibble on.

Eat Your Veggies

- Buy easy-to-prepare veggies: frozen veggie combos to steam, baby carrots, or precut broccoli and sugar peas from the salad bar.
- Keep veggies in sight, washed and trimmed, so you don't end up with limp ones in the back of the fridge.
- Add carrots and celery (even limp ones) to soup—homemade versions or from cans. Grate carrots, onions, and

zucchini into meatloaf, burgers, or soups. Add veggies to pizza and lasagna.

- Sauté green leafy veggies (spinach, chard, kale, mustard greens) with carrots and onions in olive oil to add a little sweetness to the greens.
- Drink veggie juice to add nutrients. Some dieticians say juice should be limited to one serving a day, since juice contains none of the whole veggie's valuable fiber.
- Eat your veggies even if you take vitamins. Phytochemicals can't be "duplicated and put into nutritional supplements," says Jennifer Thompson, a clinical dietician with Baylor University Medical Center.

Fruit

Now that we've eaten our veggies, let's have some fruit for dessert. Fruits have vitamins, minerals, and phytochemicals too.

Blueberries help memory, motor skills, balance, and coordination. They are full of antioxidants. Blueberries help arteries contract, which is good for blood pressure. They even reduce the damage of a stroke from a blood clot. Rats on a blueberry-enriched diet learn better than their non-blueberry eating friends.

Strawberries are filled with antioxidants and have been shown to increase memory with its chemical *fisetin*—a bioflavonoid (fisetin is also found in tomatoes, onions, oranges, apples, and kiwi).

Other **high-antioxidant fruits** (and veggies) are blackberries, cranberries, strawberries, raspberries, spinach, Brussels sprouts, plums, broccoli, beets, avocados, oranges, red grapes, red bell peppers, cherries, and kiwis. Berries from Brazil (açai) and Hawaii (goji) have been touted for high antioxidants, though they're often expensive and perishable compared to the bounty in the grocery store.

Apples, especially red ones like Red Delicious and Northern Spry, contain *phenolics*—a chemical that protects the brain from damage leading to Alzheimer's and Parkinson's disease.

Red grapes benefit brain cells and can improve cognitive function—even reverse aging of neurons, according to *Nutrition* journal. You can take supplements from grape seed extracts or the antioxidant chemical resveratrol as well.

Mice that were fed **pomegranate juice** zoomed through mazes 35 percent faster than their peers—indicating increased learning and memory in this preliminary research. Pomegranate-fed mice also had 50 percent less Alzheimer's buildup in the brain.

Spices

Will a little Indian curry help your brain? The chemical *curcumin* that makes **turmeric** yellow appears to activate a key antioxidizing enzyme that reduces plaque buildup. It also is an anti-inflammatory that fights some cancers and multiple sclerosis.

Saffron fights depression in humans, as well as improving learning and memory in animals. Saffron twice a day was as effective as Prozac in treating mild to moderate depression, according to a 2005 study in the *Journal of Ethnopharmacology.* While saffron is expensive ($8 to $12 per gram), a few threads in your cooking might make you feel better at the end of dinner.

Sage, the aptly named herb, is a potent antioxidant and anti-inflammatory. Chinese sage root contains compounds similar to Alzheimer's disease drugs, and just 50 microliters of sage oil extract significantly enhanced memory, according to research in *Pharmacological Biochemical Behavior.* Sage is a great addition to salads, in soups, even on pizza. It tastes and smells better fresh.

A whiff of **cinnamon** boosts your brain. Even cinnamon-flavored gum enhances memory, visual-motor speed, recognition, attention, and focus. Cinnamon is a wonder spice: it helps to regulate sugar levels; reduces proliferation of leukemia and lymphoma cancer cells; reduces clotting of blood platelets; acts as an antimicrobial, which means it helps with yeast infections; contains the trace mineral manganese and is a very good source of dietary fiber, iron, and calcium. Try some apples and cinnamon for a snack—especially for your kids before homework.

Caffeine

Have you had a caffeine buzz today? Eighty to 90 percent of Americans regularly consume caffeine-containing foods—coffee, tea, sodas, and chocolate—according to Johns Hopkins Medical Center. The average daily consumption in this country is about 280 mg a day; that's three 6-ounce cups of coffee or five full bottles of cola.

I'd have some coffee as I type this, but it gives me heart palpitations. Caffeine can also disrupt your sleep—even in the middle of the night. It can make you anxious, causing panic attacks for some in high doses (over 200 mg a day). Other symptoms include restlessness, rambling flow of thought and speech, digestive upset, tremors and twitching, diuresis (lots of urine), and agitation.

The average daily consumption in this country is about 280 mg a day; that's three 6-ounce cups of coffee or five full bottles of cola.

Some people have reactions when they *don't* have coffee: headache, fatigue, lack of concentration, decreased motivation, crabbiness, depression, anxiety, and flu-like symptoms. Time to order another latte? Many people drink coffee to temporarily mask the symptoms of withdrawal.

While caffeine jazzes you up, it's not "free energy," according to neurologist Dr. R. L. Kaplan, developer of the SmartKit Web site. Since *every action has an equal and opposite reaction,* ups become downs when the caffeine wears off. Caffeinated overdrive stresses your brain "hardware." Dr. Kaplan's advice: Just take the minimum caffeine to get the job done.

To reduce caffeine slowly, skip a cup a day, mix decaf with regular coffee, drink green tea, or a natural picker-upper like veggie juice. There are many ways to manage energy flow when caffeine free—stretching, exercise, and fresh air. Check out my book, *365 Energy Boosters,* for more ideas.

Chocolate

Chocolate stimulates cognitive performance, mood, and task organization, according to Dr. Bryan Raudenbush of Wheeling Jesuit University in West Virginia. The chemicals in the cacao/cocoa bean (from which chocolate is made) mimic the rush of falling in love and the altered state of marijuana. Cocoa beans also contain the feel-good chemical *flavanol*, which until recently was lost in the processing. The Mars company has been developing CocoaPro with flavanol. Or you can eat cacao nibs.

Chocolate may not be symptom free, though. It can cause headaches, restlessness, insomnia, tachycardia (rapid heart beats), agitation, and anxiety. Some of those symptoms arrive with withdrawal—when the chocolate and sugar buzz is over. Be aware of how chocolate works for you.

Green and Black Tea

Green tea has a variety of great chemicals for the brain. **Catechins** provide nerve energy, have antioxidant activity, and may be anticarcinogenic, anti-inflammatory, and antimicrobial (fights growth of bacteria, viruses, and fungi). **Polyphenols** support mood, provide antioxidants for the heart, protect against brain disorders and Parkinson's disease, and keep glucose (brain energy levels) steady. **Tannins** help the brain recover from stroke and other brain injuries. **LTheanine** may increase serotonin, dopamine, and anxiety-reducing GABA (Gamma-aminobutyric acid) levels, as well as relaxing alpha waves, the calm brain activity that occurs while resting with your eyes closed.

Green and black teas protect against the destruction of certain neurotransmitters—which is the same function as drugs that treat Alzheimer's. Dr. Daniel Amen suggests drinking two cups of tea per day, but remember, teas have caffeine, with black teas usually having more than green teas.

Other Foods and the Brain

Some common foods can do your body good. Or not.

Egg yolks contribute a brain fatty chemical called *choline* to your diet. Choline is responsible for brain health and function and can reduce the mental decline of aging and the incidence of Alzheimer's disease.

Is **alcohol** good or bad? On one hand, overuse of alcohol causes brain impairment (short term) and brain damage to the frontal lobes and ventricles (long term). In fact, individuals who had at least two drinks a day shrunk their brains by an average of 1.6 percent. Women had greater shrinkage.

On the other hand (or *in* the other hand) is a glass of red wine. Resveratrol and flavonoids found in red grapes and wine can improve cognitive function. Wine-drinking mice (they had moderate amounts) showed slower memory loss and brain cell death. Word is, if you're healthy and not addicted to alcohol, one glass of red wine (one to two glasses per day for men) can reduce the incidence of Alzheimer's disease. Grape juice has a similar effect, and perhaps dark beer.

Light alcoholic drinking (one to four drinks *a week*) can reduce risk of ischemic (clotting) strokes, while heavy drinking (three-plus per day) increases stroke risk by 45 percent, according to the Beth Israel Deaconess Medical Center. Alcohol is a blood thinner, so check with your doctor if you're taking aspirin or other thinning agents.

And **soda**? It packs a powerful punch that depletes your body of vitamin A, calcium, magnesium, and water. The high levels of phosphoric acid in soft drinks are good for cleaning a car's engine—not so good for your bone health or digestion.

How much **water** do you need? That depends on your body, weather, and activity. Sixty-four ounces of water is the general guideline, although you don't have to drink eight glasses. Water can also come from tea, fruits, and veggies. However, soda, coffee, and alcohol are diuretics—they take water from your body. A dehydrated brain thinks more slowly, so take a glug at the water fountain (about an ounce per glug).

Salt can create high blood pressure for some people, which can lead to stroke. Taste buds get hooked on salt, though you can learn to love lemon and herbs with food. Natural sea salts have more of the trace minerals your body needs, says University of Washington nutritionist Dori Khakpour.

Sugar and refined carbohydrates excite your taste buds—and brain—though your body has to produce insulin to balance it all out. After the sugar rush, there's too much insulin. You may feel spacey, weak, or anxious. Sugar and corn syrup also lead to diabetes, which sets the stage for stroke.

Nutritionist Khakpour suggests natural alternative sources, such as Succanat and Stevia, for a sweet taste. Artificial sweeteners have aroused major concerns about brain problems, although the FDA has declared the sweeteners safe to eat.

Meal Time

Many studies insist on a **breakfast** of carbs first thing, but nutritionist Dori Khakpour disagrees. Most research was funded by cereal companies, she says. The liver produces glucose between 4:00 and 7:00 a.m., so you're not as hungry when you wake. While breakfast is important for kids, she suggests adults have a large glass of water first thing, and eat nuts and fruit when hunger hits a few hours later.

To keep your brain active after **lunch,** cut down—or avoid—carbohydrates. Veggies or a salad and protein (including high-protein grains like quinoa) see you more safely through the afternoon.

Allergies and Food Intolerance

We may love food, but some food doesn't love us.

Food allergies, hypersensitivity, or intolerance can create reactions to your meals. Orange juice might give you a rash, peanuts a deathly shock. But the link between food allergy and brain fog may not be as visible.

While allergies produce antibodies to a food (that's the deadly reaction to strawberries or nuts), food intolerance can develop over time, related to different organs of your body.

I have an autoimmune reaction that lowers my platelets and made me bruised, tired, and sick. A normal platelet count is 150,000 to 450,000 platelets per microliter—mine were 28,000. My doctor suggested I stop eating wheat, and my platelets went up to 80,000 within weeks; they have stayed up for two years.

Brain Allergies?

The brain's a good organ. And it can be affected by your diet. Nutritionists and cutting-edge medical providers think certain foods can cause "brain allergies"—brain fog, agitation, anxiety, weepiness, depression, attention deficit disorder (ADD), panic, nightmares, paranoia—a whole range of psychological, emotional, or neurological symptoms.

High-intolerance foods include milk, eggs, nuts, wheat (and glutenous grains), beef, corn, tomatoes, citrus foods, and soy as well as food additives and colorings. Some say that sugar and yeast foods trigger *Candida*, an overgrowth of yeast in the body, which causes brain fog, or a perpetual "hung-over feeling." In the great irony of bodies, some people crave the foods they're most allergic to.

An allergist can determine if you have an immune response. Food sensitivities may require an elimination diet, says Dr. Fernando Vega, founder of Seattle Healing Arts. Eat low-allergen foods, including lamb, turkey, rice, millet, squash, and others. Eliminate foods such as dairy, gluten, alcohol, caffeine, sugar, and others your provider may suggest. Drink at least two quarts of water per day. Or use a nutrition supplement. When symptoms abate, add one possibly allergic food at a time, and note reactions in a food diary. A medical provider (doctor, nutritionist, ARNP [advanced registered nurse practitioner]) can guide you through this.

What can you eat if you discover a food intolerance? Since so many people have intolerances, companies have developed healthy new products that taste good (my daughter tries to scarf my gluten-free ginger snaps).

Should You Take Supplements?

Americans swallow capsules to enhance diet, moods, or thinking. Are we avant-garde or guinea pigs?

> Don't overdose on minerals—or vitamins.
> Some can be toxic in large amounts.

Some say that a whole-food diet is all you need. Others say supplements are nutritional research and development, first used in alternative therapy and later adapted by traditional medical providers. Still others say they're a way for companies to make a fast buck from people's desire for better health.

If you choose to take supplements—and there are good reasons to, unless you adhere to a pristine diet—find reliable sources for your information: doctor, naturopath, or nutritionist; health newsletters such the *Harvard* or the *Berkeley*

Wellness Health Letter; Web sites such as the University of Maryland Complementary Medicine (*www.umm.edu/altmed/*) or Dr. Weil (*www.drweil.com*). Although Dr. Weil sells supplements, he has a history of careful research in making his recommendations. These sources can confirm what you hear from well-meaning friends or the clerk at the health food store.

Don't overdose on minerals—or vitamins. Some, like selenium, can be toxic in large amounts.

Taking Supplements

Before you take a supplement, check with your doctor. Supplements can affect many parts of the body beyond the ones indicated on the label. Also, try one new supplement at a time, so you can monitor your body's reactions. Your body tells you what's making a difference.

Brain Supplements

The supplements listed here include vitamins, minerals, fish oils, foods, and herbs that have been widely researched to help with brain, heart (good for the brain), and stress. Suggested adult dosages are from Drs. Andrew Weil or Daniel Amen.

- **Multiple vitamins and minerals** can boost poor diets, although they don't substitute for healthy eating. You may want to add a **B-complex** as well. Multivitamins or B-complex supplements would include 400–800 mcg of folate, 50 mg of B-6, and 500–1000 mcg of B-12.
- **Vitamin C.** New research shows that bodies can't absorb more than 250 mg of vitamin C per day, the amount Dr. Weil recommends. Some nutritionists suggest buffered vitamin C (which includes minerals) for better absorption.
- **Vitamin E.** Suggested dosage: 100 International Units (IU) twice a day, though not the dl (synthetic) form, says Dr. Amen.
- **Boron.** Beer, wine, body-building supplements, and tap water in certain locations can provide boron. Supplements are usually dosed at 3 mg per day.
- **Iron.** Include some vitamin C with iron to absorb it better—and don't take calcium at the same time, as it blocks absorption. Whole food supplements may be easier to digest, say some nutritionists.
- **Coenzyme Q10 (coQ10)** is part of the energy-producing mitochondria of the cell, acts as an antioxidant, and helps produce ATP (adenosine triphosphate), a molecule that serves as the cells' major energy source. CoQ10 is good for blood

pressure, the heart, and it has been shown to help with Alzheimer's and Parkinson's disease. Suggested dosage: 60–120 mg per day.

- **Acetyl-L-Carnitine (ALC).** Preliminary research suggests that ALC may help stimulate neural transmission and slow the decline of Alzheimer's. Along with coQ10, it may energize brain cells. Suggested dosage: 500–1500 mg per day.
- **Alpha-lipoic acid** works with other antioxidants such as vitamins C and E to prevent cell damage. It can pass easily into the brain, helps protect brain and nerve tissue, and may help treat stroke and other brain disorders. You can get alpha-lipoic acid from spinach, broccoli, beef, and Brewer's yeast. Suggested supplement dosage: 100–200 mg per day.
- **Ginkgo biloba,** from the Chinese gingko tree, is a well-used and well-studied antioxidant. It enhances circulation, cognitive function, memory, and concentration. It appears to slow the progression of early Alzheimer's disease. Ginkgo is a blood thinner. Suggested dosage: 60–120 milligrams twice a day with food. It may take six to eight weeks to build its effect.
- The natural nutrient **phosphatidylserine** is a component of nerve cell membranes. It appears to increase brain activity and cognition, support mood,

and reduce the damage of early Alzheimer's. Suggested dosage: 100–300 mg per day for those at risk for dementia or memory problems.

- Organic acid **taurine** interacts with the thalamus—the regulatory area of the brain. Taurine is often included in energy drinks such as Red Bull, although scientists think it actually has a sedating effect on the brain. Dosage is about 1 to 3 grams per day, according to Dr. Michael Lam.

- **Quercetin** is a flavonoid that not only is responsible for the colors of many fruits and vegetables, but provides many health-promoting benefits. Among its roles as an antioxidant and in fighting allergies, quercetin reduces cholesterol and helps the heart—both good for the brain. You can get it from foods such as citrus fruits, apples, onions, parsley, tea, red wine, olive oil, grapes, dark cherries, and dark berries, and also from supplements. Dosage: 100 to 250 mg three times per day, though it can be higher to treat allergies or other illnesses.

- Some recommend low doses of the **mineral lithium** for moods and nerve health, even to prevent Alzheimer's. However research is still in its early stages, and toxicity can occur with over-dosage. Dr. Jonathan Wright, author of *Dr. Wright's Guide to Healing with Nutrition,* recommends taking low-dose lithium, 5 milligrams of lithium aspartate or lithium orotate available from a some natural food stores and compounding pharmacies.

Supplements for Stress

Stress, depression, and mood disorders can put the brain in overdrive. While you can physically destress and calm yourself (see chapter 4), supplements may help ease tension. Always check with your doctor's office or medical provider to monitor dosage, just as you do for prescribed medications. Combining antidepressant supplements and/or pills is not recommended.

- **GABA (Gamma-aminobutyric acid)** can calm temper and anxiety by stabilizing the tendency of nerve cells to fire erratically or excessively, says Dr. Amen. He suggests taking 250–1500 mg daily in two or three doses.
- **SAMe (S-adenosylmethionine)** is a natural antidepressant for mild to moderate depression that has been shown to work as well as pharmaceutical ones. However, it's not suggested for individuals with bipolar disorder. Suggested dosage: 200–400 mg two to four times a day.
- **St. John's Wort,** a cheery, yellow flowering herb that blooms around the summer solstice, has been shown

to help with mild to moderate depression. It increases sun sensitivity, may decrease the effectiveness of birth control pills, and has contraindications with other disorders and medications. Suggested dosage: 0.3 percent hypericin (the active ingredient in St. John's Wort), taken as 300 mg three times a day (or 600 mg in the morning, and 300 at night).

- **5-HTP,** a controversial supplement, is a building block for serotonin, which regulates mood and sleep, providing antidepressant effects. Dosage is 50–100 mg two or three times a day.

- **Inositol** seems to help neurons better use the neurotransmitter serotonin. Preliminary research suggests it helps with mild depression, negative thoughts, and rigid thinking, according to Dr. Amen. The dose is up to 18 grams a day.

- **Valerian** is a traditional herb used for anxiety, muscle relaxation, and sleeping. It appears to have a lower potential for addiction, though the rules for prescription medication apply to valerian: don't take it with alcohol or other prescriptive tranquilizers, and not while pregnant or breastfeeding. The recommended dose is 150–450 mg in capsules or tea.

Making Changes

How do you change familiar, comforting, not-so healthy habits into the brain-health diet? Jump in cold turkey—easier to do alone, harder if you eat with kids or traditional American diners.

Or you can change one habit at a time to adjust your taste buds. Even small changes make a big difference over time: a pilot makes a minor adjustment in Chicago and ends up in Phoenix instead of Fairbanks.

Easy Steps

Follow these recommendations from nutritionists at Bastyr University, a renowned school for naturopaths:

- Reduce saturated fats and eliminate trans fats
- Eat as much omega-3-rich sources as you can
- Add antioxidants to your diet, from food if possible
- Buy organic whenever possible to reduce toxins
- Add an extra veggie a day
- Have fruit and nuts for a late breakfast
- Make lunch your healthiest meal
- Try a new grain such as millet

Clear out food you want to avoid—and pictures and commercials of it. Give yourself twenty-one days to help your new habit to entrench.

If you fall face first into a pile of cupcakes, remember you are practicing a new routine. You fell when you first wanted to ride a bike— then you got back on and learned to whiz down the block. Practice your new relationship with food.

Enjoy the wisdom of your body. And enjoy what you eat!

7

Meditation and a Bigger Perspective

Less Is More

Don't believe everything you think.

—Bumper sticker

Claude was up to his eyebrows in stress. As manager of the county engineering department, his days were full of politics and deadlines. He carried tension in his shoulders, had high blood pressure, and was easily distracted.

"Try meditation," suggested his doctor at a routine physical exam.

Claude couldn't figure out how sitting on a pillow and staring at his navel could help. But he could spare a few Wednesday nights for a beginning meditation class.

He was glad to find chairs in the classroom. And students who seemed just like him: stressed-out achievers. The teacher asked them to sit and close their eyes. She suggested they notice the body on the chair and let the attention drift toward the breath. "You can notice it in your nose, your chest, your abdomen."

The first few breaths were good. Claude remembered he had a body. Then he was antsy to check his email, stretch, call his sweetheart . . . anything other than just breathe.

"Thoughts naturally arise," the teacher continued. "Let them go, just like clouds as you come back to the breath."

Claude noticed his chest rise and fall. "Awareness settles on the inhale," said the teacher. "It may help to think the words 'breathing in' as you inhale . . . and the words 'breathing out' on the exhale."

Claude felt his shoulders let go. Deadlines faded. Meditation wasn't as weird as he thought.

Over the weeks of class, Claude surprised himself. He could sit and "do nothing" for 30, even 40 minutes. Some moments were hard—his mind was a maze of incomplete project specs and budgets. Then the teacher's voice reminded him to come back to the breath.

Meditation relaxed his body and his mind. He bought a green meditation cushion and set up a spot the bedroom. He'd definitely practice every day, he thought.

However when the class ended, Claude had to drag himself to the cushion at home. He knew meditation helped. But practicing it? He was too busy.

What Is Meditation?

Meditation is a natural resting state where you also remain alert. It is any activity that "keeps the attention pleasantly anchored in the present moment," says Dr. Joan Borysenko, author of *Minding the Body, Mending the Mind.*

You naturally shift into a meditative state when you're learning, healing, or renewing. You might notice it when you walk on the beach, get massage, or sip a slow cup of tea. Thoughts and emotions come and go as you return focus to the waves or your relaxation.

Even if you're miles from a beach, you can still practice the meditative state. A variety of techniques, from sitting to movement, allow you to renew while awake. This renewal energizes the brain; it increases focus, memory, creativity, and reduces stress. Similar benefits occur with prayer.

If meditation feels great, why can it be difficult at times? The conscious mind resists letting go. It would rather plan, analyze, or sleep than focus on the moment. Over time, though, even the conscious mind discovers benefits from relaxed awareness in the body, emotions, and brain.

Meditation and the Brain

Meditation doesn't mean 20 minutes of instant happiness (or else there'd be more meditation centers than Starbucks), though it does change the brain activity of the left-prefrontal cortex—associated with positive emotions. That's true for practiced meditators and even those new to meditation, said researcher Richard Davidson.

Benefits of Meditation

Scientists have discovered that meditation and prayer change brainwaves and activity under the skull. While most of the research has been on meditation, intensive prayer has been shown to have similar results.

In the **body,** meditation:

- Increases blood flow, slows the heart rate, and reduces blood pressure

- Decreases muscle tension and body pain
- Helps with post-operative healing, premenstrual syndrome, and chronic diseases such as allergies and arthritis
- Enhances the immune system, reduces activity of viruses, and increases "natural killer-cells" which attack bacteria and cancer cells
- Improves health and positive health habits, including increasing exercise tolerance and decreasing cigarette, alcohol, and drug abuse

In the **brain**, meditation:

- Organizes brain functioning
- Improves cognitive function, focus, perception, and memory
- Improves productivity, intelligence, and creativity

With **emotions**, meditation:

- Reduces anxiety attacks by lowering blood lactate levels
- Builds self-confidence
- Increases response time for emotional reactivity—so you think before you blow your stack

- Increases serotonin production (a neurotransmitter that boosts mood)
- Reduces depression

Dr. Richard Davidson, neuroscientist at the University of Wisconsin, pioneered research on the brain and meditation. He wired novice meditators and Buddhist monks with a spaghetti-like mesh of 256 electric sensors. Novice meditators had taken a class and had meditated for 30 minutes a day for several weeks, while the experienced monks had meditated for 10,000 to 50,000 hours over 15 to 40 years.

During meditation, both groups created high-frequency gamma brainwaves. These brainwaves are the crème de la crème for brainwave surfing—they synchronize diverse brain activity and heighten higher mental awareness. The gamma waves continued to remain strong between meditation sessions for the expert Buddhist monks.

Along with generating brainwaves, meditation heightened activity in specific regions in the brain. By using functional MRIs (magnetic resonance imaging) to detect body changes, Dr. Davidson uncovered greater activity for both novice and experienced meditators in areas that monitor emotions, plan movements, and generate positive feelings. The monks' brains also had enhanced neural coordination for focus, memory, learning and consciousness. "Our findings clearly indicate that meditation can change the function of the brain in an enduring way," said Dr. Davidson at a neuroscience conference with the Dalai Lama.

Meditation can change the function of the brain in an enduring way.

Prayer and spiritual activity also show similar changes, according to Dr. Andrew Newberg of the University of Pennsylvania, who monitored brain activity of praying Franciscan nuns. Prayer and meditation don't change the brain instantaneously. Having a gentle approach and willingness to practice (even if you just sit for 5 minutes on busy days) lay the foundation.

How to Meditate

- **Sit** on a cushion or chair with a straight back. If possible, avoid leaning into back cushions.
- **Close your eyes,** or let them gently focus on the wall or floor a few feet ahead.
- **Settle.** Let your attention alight on your body.
- **Focus.** Use your breath, a mantra (repeated phrase), loving kindness, or the sounds around you.
- **Return to the focus.** Notice when thoughts, emotions, and irritations arise, then return to your focus.

Meditation Techniques

How many ways are there to meditate? As many as letters on this page. You can focus on any sensation: a cloud moving in the sky, the repetition of a phrase, or mindful walk. You can sit and breathe, pray, get centered in your body, or do qi gong. You can find enlightening meditation traditions in Christianity, Islam (Sufi), and Jewish (Kabbalah) as well as traditional Buddhism and Hinduism.

No matter which method you chose, stay with it for a few weeks or months instead of switching from one to another, to see how it connects.

- **Breathe.** It's an age-old meditation. Your breath is always there, providing a soft rhythm and connection to life. Start by exhaling, and then naturally inhale. Notice the flow of breath in your nostrils, chest, or abdomen. To deepen the meditation, turn your eyes toward your heart, even if they're closed. Let your awareness settle on just this one breath, suggests teacher Sharon Salzburg, then just the next one. Perhaps you'll experience the fullness of the lungs, pauses between inhale and exhale, emptiness as you breathe out. Some individuals like to mentally repeat a phrase— "Breathing in . . . Breathing out . . ."—for each inhale or exhale. Or you can count each breath cycle until you reach ten breaths, then start over again.

- **Chant.** It intensifies focus on the breath. Chant a phrase, prayer, the sound of *om.*
- **Contemplate** an object that inspires you from nature, religion, or spiritual connection. "Imagine, sense or feel the essential truth of this image," say Joel and Michelle Levey, authors of several books on meditation.
- **Repeat a mantra** (phrase) or **prayer** in your head. It's a powerful form of concentration. The phrase can be a prayer or inspiration such as "Thy will be done," "Shalom," or "Peace." Or repeat prayers, such as a Sufi Zikr, the *Sh'ma,* the rosary, or *Om Mani Padme Hum.*
- **Concentrate** on an image. Could be a cross, Star of David, image of Buddha, a seashell. It could be a real item or one in your mind. This teaches you to hold attention on one object, says Ragini Michaels, NLP trainer, without being distracted by other sensory input.
- In **Loving-Kindness** or **Metta Meditation,** you repeat compassionate phrases in your mind. Start with yourself, then expand to those you love, those you know, those you dislike, and all beings in the world. Find compassionate phrases that resonate for you, suggests Sharon Salzburg, such as "May you be happy," "May you be healthy," "May you be safe,"

"May you live in peace." During retreats, I've done Loving-Kindness Meditation while walking, sending these phrases to those I've passed, changing the sense of myself in the world.

- In **mindful sitting**, you expand your focus beyond breath to include the larger world. "About 25% of your attention is on breathing and the other 75% on the feeling of spacious mindfulness," says Dr. Borysenko. The purpose is to let thoughts, sensations, emotions, and sounds arise and pass away. You learn to let each moment be, without clinging to it or avoiding it.

- **Walking meditation** focuses on how your body moves and balances. As you walk, your become aware of shifting weight, lifting the heel, lifting the toes, moving the foot through space, placing it, shifting weight. . . . During meditation retreats, hundreds of people inch past rose bushes, not smelling the flowers but concentrating on each step. You can also practice a fast walking meditation. Become aware of the movement of a single foot, then the other foot. Or repeat "Step, step, step" as you walk.

- **Movement Meditation.** These sessions involve repetitive movements, often with music. There are CDs and classes for many forms, including *tai chi,* Osho active meditations (rhythmic, repeated movement), or *qi gong.*

- **Mindful Sensations.** Meditate on what you do in each moment—eating, drinking, touch, sounds. In *mindful eating,* look, smell, and taste just one slice of a navel orange. Notice the texture, citrus smell, light reflected on the slices, the feel before your bite releases the juices. In *sound meditation,* become aware of loud and soft, silence and noise. Or start with the sounds farthest away—airplanes or cars—and move in to hear sounds in the other room or your breath. Minds get curious about sounds. Is the *taptaptap* a dripping faucet or a loose shingle on the roof? Let sounds and silence enter your ears. You may find focus without perfect quiet.
- **Visualizations.** Some types of meditation encourage visualizations to tune into or heal the body, such as imagining a flow of energy through the body and the seven chakras, energy centers of the body. Some Buddhist meditation traditions, such as Tibetan, include visualization as part of the path. Some teachers say that repeating the same visualization in each meditation session can strengthen the mind's concentration. However, most teachers encourage students to spend a good deal of time—perhaps years—on mindful focus on the breath before expanding to visualization.

Returning to the Mind

Your mind and body may fill the meditation time with various sensations: review of daily experiences, relaxation, relief, releasing emotions, antsy-ness, creativity, boredom, momentary sense of quiet and peace, sleepiness or dreamy images, and a new level of awareness.

You may spend the entire 30 minutes enjoying the sensation of your breath. Or you may notice your breath once or twice, figure out the agenda for your board meeting, then turn awareness to your breath again. That's also meditation—returning to notice the mind.

Here are some gentle approaches to meditation:

- **Let yourself be.** Emotions, sensations, and thoughts arise and fall. It doesn't help to try to control, slow down, or edit them.
- **Train your wandering mind.** Think of meditation like strengthening your triceps at the gym. Each "rep" means improving your ability to focus, which reduces the impact of worries and outside influences. Instead, label the thought as a *thought* or *memory, plan, blame.* Then return to the breath or other object of contemplation.
- **Be kind to your mind.** Even when your mind frustrates you, don't berate it or yell at it. Instead, give your mind gentle reminders: "Time to focus now . . . and now . . . and now."

- **Take your time.** You can relax for just a few breaths (meditation teacher Sally Kempton calls them mini-meditations). However, you'll find deeper levels of release with time. It's just like vacation: one day is nice, a week is much better. Experienced meditators, including the Dalai Lama, often need 20 to 30 minutes to detach from the chattering mind. And give yourself at least a month to make meditation a meaningful habit.
- **Stay the course.** Practice one form of mediation to focus the mind. If you jump from technique to technique (in the hopes that one of them will enlighten you), you distract yourself. However, listen to your body. If a technique feels distressing the first few times you practice it, find another one that connects better.
- **Explore possibilities.** Many experienced meditators stay with one technique for years or decades. Others find it useful to add a new technique after they've developed a practice in one area, letting meditation evolve as they grow.

Other Issues

Other questions may arise for beginning meditators.

Where do you meditate? Most instructors recommend an upright posture. Meditation benches (supported kneeling) or thick zafu (round, fabric) cushions help position your pelvis to support your spine. However, chairs work fine as well. Even the car will do in a pinch.

How do you deal with inevitable irritations that arise from sitting still? Notice what the sensation actually feels like. Does it fade, spread, or fluctuate over time? Do urgent stories go along with the sensation? "I won't be able to walk if I don't move my legs now." Move slowly with awareness when you change position.

What about anger, sadness, or other emotions that persist? Instead of repeating stories in your mind ("How could my cousin talk to me that way?"), notice your sensory experiences. Are you clutching in the stomach, wrinkling your brow? Watch as sensations change—they usually do. Try the techniques in chapter 2, including Tapas Acupressure Technique, or Sally Kempton's techniques in chapter 4 to reduce the emotional charge.

While sleepiness may be part of relaxing in meditation, traditional paths encourage awareness of even your sleepy mind in meditation. It may help to press your tongue to the roof of your mouth or open your eyes. As an alternative, you can try a movement meditation—or take a brief nap before you begin sitting.

☆ Meditation Boosters ☆

The boosters that follow help you start or deepen your meditation practice. I've included a range of suggestions—but don't try them all at once. Incorporate those that resonate. Check back if they don't feel right after a week or more of practice. As Dr. Borysenko said to me, "No matter what kind of meditation you do, you get to the same place."

These suggestions come from the works of Sally Kempton (*The Heart of Meditation*), Joel and Michelle Levey (*Luminous Mind*), Camille and Lorin Roche (*Meditation Made Easy*), Sharon Salzburg (*Lovingkindness Meditation*), Joan Borysenko (*Mending the Body, Mending the Mind*), Ragini Michaels (*Facticity*), as well as my own experience.

Create a Structure and a Habit

A structure helps instill meditation routine. That can include establishing a special place, meditating at the same time each day, having a ritual for your practice, and finding a community in a class or group.

- **Create a clear space.** Set up a corner or room decorated with reminders that "energize the heart," suggest the Leveys. But don't wait for the perfect space. Find an area with few distractions (it's harder to let go when there are baskets of laundry at your feet). Straighten up a room. Or face your chair or cushion toward the wall. Turn off the phone and put a sign on the door so you won't be disturbed until you're done.

- **Attend to the body.** Start with how you position your body. It's easier to remain alert if you keep your spine vertical. Sit comfortably on a chair, cross-legged on a cushion, or kneel on a meditation bench. Then let your awareness rest with your body. Relax as you release your muscles from head to toes or visualize light flowing through your body. Try yoga (which was developed to increase the ability to meditate) before you sit. Walking or movement meditation is a great alternative to sitting.

- **Release.** As you begin to relax, you may feel release phenomena—twitches, gurgling stomach, quivery body, or mental images. Over time, these reservoirs of accumulated stress will drain, say the Leveys. You will feel clearer and better able to handle daily challenges.

- **Balance relaxation and alertness.** Sometimes you feel sleepy in meditation, sometimes fidgety. You can balance the energy. To be more alert, keep your eyes softly open, press the tongue to the roof of the mouth, or straighten the spine. To relax, focus on a calm part of the body or allow the tense sensations dissipate.

- **An inner smile.** Thich Nhat Hahn, a renowned Vietnamese Zen Buddhist teacher, encourages an inner smile during meditation and daily life. Having a gentle inner smile—in the eyes and mouth—inflects a peaceful perspective.

- **Dedication and ritual.** As you begin a session, remember your purpose for meditation, offer a prayer of gratitude, or envision joining meditators around the world. At the end of your practice, imagine your sense of peace radiating through your day and the Earth.

More Meditation Suggestions

Here are a few other meditation suggestions to explore.

- Focus on the pauses between breaths. Focus on the spaces between thoughts.
- Become aware of your heartbeat.
- Contemplate how emptiness (space between atoms) is part of everything.
- Notice meditation in lovemaking as you come back to focus on the body.
- Contemplate impermanence: everything changes. That helps to surf the tides of life.

- Ask yourself, "Who am I?" Ask again when you watch your thoughts . . . who's watching?

  When you watch your thoughts and ask who's watching, you open to a bigger perspective.

Bigger Perspectives

Look out the window—or in a mirror—to witness a bigger perspective on life. Night and day, summer and winter, youth and aging are all beyond human direction. Even California celebrities can't protect their multimillion-dollar homes from wildfires.

People describe this bigger force with a variety of concepts: God, science, nature, Jesus, Allah, Christlike or Buddhalike nature, deeper wisdom, Goddess, Beloved, or Essence. Differences in concepts generate arguments or wars. However, the internal experience of connection seems universal.

While we may never determine whether God or some divine presence exists beyond our inner consciousness, connecting to something larger affects the brain. Dr. Andrew Newberg says that "religious or spiritual experiences do seem to be among the more complex sets of experiences" in the whole brain.

This bigger perspective also helps the brain by reducing stress. "Spirituality gives you a purpose for living," says Dr. Todd Clements, a psychiatrist who has monitored brains with

SPECT scans (single photon emission computed tomography). He says spirituality provides hope, calms anxiety and fear, and lends an optimism to life.

Whether you're a cynic, atheist, or already hold a bigger perspective, you can deepen your connection to the greater flow in life. Some of the boosters that follow use images of a personalized connection, described as Essence or Essential Self. Or you can imagine your connection with nature or community. Find the path that works for you and your brain.

> Spirituality provides hope, calms anxiety and fear, and lends an optimism to life.

☆ Boosters: Imagine Essence ☆

These guidelines help you imagine interaction with your Essence (or whatever you chose to call this personal connection).

- **Visualize a place** to meet your Essence. Imagine a detailed scene, using sight, touch, smell, hearing, and taste. It could be a spot by the ocean where you feel the sand under your feet, smell the air, hear the waves, and taste the salty water. Or try a tree house in the mountains where you touch the wood, hear birds, smell pine sap, and taste fresh water. Choose whatever place feels right; you can always change it later.

- **Imagine your Essence.** Let the image of your Essence arise in a door or around a bend. You might sense a color or shape or see a clear image. Notice what details you can: size, movement, heat, sounds, or words. Perhaps your Essence has a "gift" or image for you. Do any areas of your body feel connected or changed by this visualization? You may feel warmer in your heart, more relaxed in your forehead, or more expansive. Remembering these sensations will help you reconnect to your Essence in the future.

- **Talk and pray.** Have a conversation with your Essence through words, images, or a feeling. Or use a familiar prayer, a poem, or words from a holy book. Express a dilemma, listen for wisdom, and see your life from a bigger perspective. You can also move as you pray, expressing concerns from your smaller self, then stepping back and speak from the wisdom of Essence.

Appreciate and Connect

- **Be grateful.** The attitude of gratitude increases optimism and longevity. It also changes brain habits. Be grateful for what you have: "Thank you for the sunset, my kids, my computer." And be thankful for actions, for being alive: "I appreciate seeing the sunset, loving my kids, rebooting my computer." Gratitude is a great lullaby before you go to sleep.

- **Dance and sing.** Movement and singing—especially with others—can open the body to a spiritual connection. Try Christmas carols, blessings, folk dances, and moving prayer.

- **Give.** Compassion makes complex frontal brain structures come alive. Giving makes you feel grateful and reminds you that everyone is part of the larger flow of life.

Prayer and Spiritual Connection

Prayer and spiritual connection give a bigger perspective.

- **Spend time with people** in church, synagogue, mosque, or meditation sangha to reduce emotional isolation.
- **Ask for help in prayer.** Assistance comes from many places when you're open for it.
- **Walk in nature.** You'll see the cycles of life, diversity in patterns, and evidence of a force greater than the emotional mind.

Take a Break

- Want to increase your spiritual connection? Stop. Exhale. . . . Inhale. . . . Exhale. . . . You'd be surprised how one focused breath can change your morning.
- Take time each day to pray or meditate. You will become more aware of life—and get more done.
- Take a Sabbath day. Eliminate some doings for the day, such as spending money, laundry, computer and TV. Instead, pray, rest, have a special walk, and connect with others.
- Spend a half-day each week with a mini-personal retreat of longer meditations, yoga, and reading.
- Go on an organized retreat. Meditation groups and religions offer daily, weekend, weekly, and month-long retreats that are powerful experiences.

Forgetting and Remembering

We naturally get caught up in daily events. The bigger perspective—even the breath—gets lost in the shuffle. "Forgetfulness will arise like a smoke screen," says Ragini Michaels. It's just part of being human.

That's what happened to Claude when his beginning meditation classes ended. Daily stress made it hard to clear out time to meditate at home.

However Claude didn't give up. He'd sit for just a few minutes each day . . . then the urge to sit a little longer arose. It felt good, even if part of his mind still thought about his email.

Over the months, his "just a few minutes" became 10 minutes, then 20 or 30. To his surprise, he became a regular meditator. He felt less driven by his mind, its desires and irritations. Instead, he sensed a connection to something larger, the natural flow of life with its cycle of seasons and even his breath. Claude's blood pressure dropped, and he could let go of worrying about work when he wasn't there. On days when he was too busy to sit, he noticed his higher reactivity—and so did his staff.

While meditation didn't cure all his problems, it made him better at handling them. Or letting them go.

Claude found a good use for the brain.

Conclusion

Here you are, at the end of the book, with new perspectives on your brain. It's a wonderful brain you have there: your ability to learn, to grow new neurons, the flow of emotions. And you can enhance that giant, jellied walnut under your spine. Because brains are so flexible and alive, even those with 140 IQs can help their brains work better.

Perhaps you know what boosters you want to try. For others, it's a question of where to start. Check out this Wheel of the Brain.

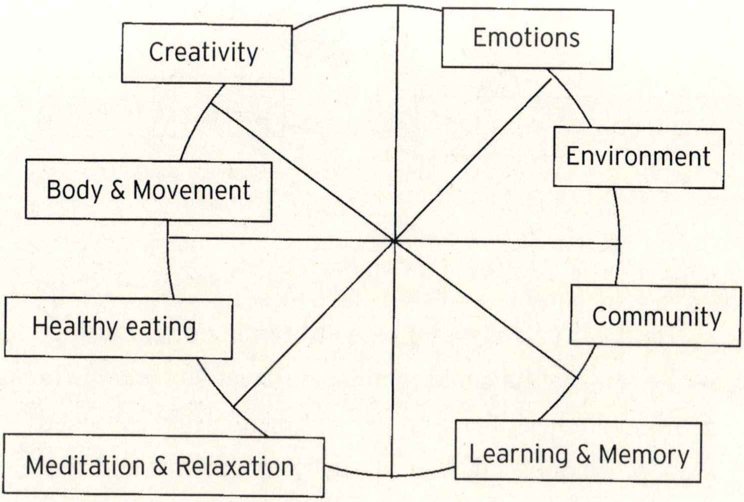

Fill in the areas based on your perception of strengths. Then you'll find where you could support your brain. For instance, Eric, an office worker, filled it in like this:

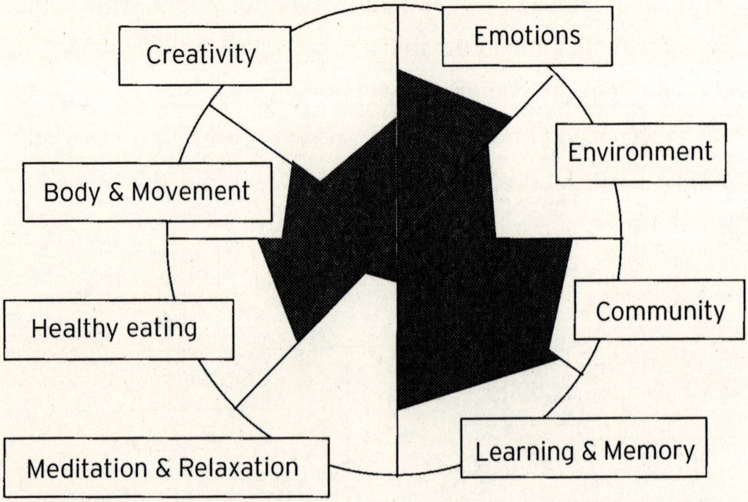

He doesn't have problems with learning or exercising . . . but he saw that he could increase his creativity and make his environment healthier. And perhaps meditate for a moment or two. So Eric took out his old, dusty watercolors and painted the glass of water on the table. Then he went outside (where he stopped using herbicides) and drew the cherry tree. His brain felt bigger somehow, just for that half-hour.

Stretch your brain each day—each hour—by breathing, stretching, remembering, challenging, touching, feeling, laughing, crying, hearing, being, and being grateful.

Your hundred billion neurons will thank you for noticing.

Bibliography and Resources

Books

Daniel Amen. *Making a Good Brain Great: The Amen Clinic Program for Achieving and Sustaining Optimal Mental Performance.* New York: Harmony Books, 2005.

Nancy Andreasen, M.D. *The Creating Brain: the Neuroscience of Genius.* New York: Dana Press, 2005.

Sharon Begley. *Train Your Mind, Change Your Brain.* New York: Ballantine Books, 2007.

Joan Borysenko, PhD. *Minding the Body, Mending the Mind.* Cambridge, MA: Da Capo Press, 2007.

Julia Cameron. *The Artist's Way: A Spiritual Path to Higher Creativity.* New York: Tarcher/Penguin, 2002.

Rick Carson. *Taming Your Gremlin: A Surprisingly Simple Method for Getting Out of Your Own Way.* New York: Quill, 2003.

Jean Carper. *Your Miracle Brain.* New York: HarperCollins, 2000.

Marla Cilley. *Sink Reflections.* New York: Bantam Books, 2002.

Norman Cousins. *Anatomy of an Illness as Perceived by the Patient.* New York: Norton, 1979.

Gavin De Becker. *The Gift of Fear: And Other Survival Signals That Protect Us from Violence.* New York: Dell, 1999.

Donna Eden. *Energy Medicine: Balance Your Body's Energies for Optimum Health, Joy, and Vitality.* New York: Tarcher/Penguin, 1999.

Paul Ekman. *Emotions Revealed: Recognizing Faces and Feelings to Improve Communication and Emotional Life.* New York: Henry Holt, 2004.

Tapas Fleming. *You Can Heal Now: The Tapas Acupressure Techniques (TAT).* Redondo Beach, CA: TAT International, 1999.

Howard Gardner. *Multiple Intelligences: New Horizons.* New York: Basic Books, 2006.

Shakti Gawain. *Creative Visualization.* Novato, CA: Nataraj Pub./New World Library, 2002.

Daniel Goleman. *Social Intelligence.* New York: Bantam Books, 2006.

Temple Grandin. *Unwritten Rules of Social Relationships.* Arlington, TX: Future Horizons, 2005.

Byron Katie. *Loving What Is: Four Questions That Can Change Your Life.* New York: Crown, 2002.

Sally Kempton (Swami Durgananda). *The Heart of Meditation: Pathways to a Deeper Experience.* South Fallsburg, NY: SYDA Foundation, 2002.

Jack Kornfield. *After the Ecstasy, the Laundry: How the Heart Grows Wise on the Spiritual Path.* New York: Bantam Books, 2001.

Anne Lamott. *Bird by Bird: Some Instructions on Writing and Life.* New York : Anchor Books, 1995.

Joel and Michelle Levey. *Luminous Mind.* San Francisco: Conari Press, 2006.

Priscilla Long. *Begin Again: The Portable Mentor for Practicing Writers.* (forthcoming)

Eric Maisel. *Ten Zen Seconds*. Naperville, IL: Sourcebooks, 2007.

Ragini Elizabeth Michaels. *Facticity: A Door to Mental Health and Beyond*. Seattle, WA: Facticity Trainings, 1991.

Marvin Minsky, M.D. *Society of Mind*. New York: Simon and Schuster, 1988.

Patricia Potter-Efron and Ronald Potter-Effron. *Letting Go of Shame*. Center City, MN: Hazelden, 1996.

Steven Pratt and Kathy Matthews, *Superfoods Rx: Fourteen Foods Proven to Change Your Life*. New York: HarperCollins, 2007.

John Ratey. *A User's Guide to the Brain: Perception, Attention, and the Four Theaters of the Brain*. New York: Pantheon, 2001.

Lorin Roche. *Meditation Made Easy*. New York: Harper San Francisco, 1998.

Sharon Salzberg. *Lovingkindness: The Revolutionary Art of Happiness*. Boston, London: Shambhala, 2004, 1995.

Susannah Seton and Sondra Kornblatt. *365 Energy Boosters*. San Francisco: Conari Press, 2005.

Renna Shesso. *Math for Mystics : From the Fibonacci Sequence to Luna's Labyrinth to the Golden Sections and Other Secrets of Sacred Geometry*. San Francisco: Red Wheel/Weiser, 2007.

Andrew Weil, M.D., and Gary Small, M.D. *The Healthy Brain Kit*. Louisville, CO: Sounds True, 2007.

John Wright, *Dr. Wright's Guide to Healing with Nutrition*. New York: McGraw-Hill, 1990.

Web sites

cosmeticsdatabase.com (Environmental Working Group Cosmetics Database)

csrees.usda.gov/Extension (state extension offices)

the-dma.org/consumers/offmailinglist.html (Direct Marketing Association's Mail Preference Service)

donotcall.gov (eliminate junk calls).

drweil.com (Dr. Andrew Weil, alternative medicine)

enneagraminstitute.com (Enneagram: theory of nine personality types)

faculty.washington.edu/chudler/index1.html (Neuroscience for Kids—and adults, too)

flylady.com (organizing your home)

foodnews.org/ (Environmental Working Group—food)

freerice.com (vocabulary and hunger-support)

ldrc.ca/projects/miinventory/miinventory.php (multiple intelligence strengths)

mbayaq.org/cr/seafoodwatch.asp (Seafood Watch Program from the Monterey Bay Aquarium)

mcphee.com (Archie McPhee's toys and amusements)

myersbriggs.org (Myers Briggs test)

napo.net (National Association of Professional Organizers)

oceansalive.org (Oceans Alive easy-to use list of safe fish)

pollutioninpeople.org (toxic chemicals in humans)

psy.vanderbilt.edu/faculty/bachorowski/laugh.htm. (recorded laughs)

restfulinsomnia.com (how to renew when you can't sleep)

smart-kit.com (online puzzles and brain games)

tatlife.com (Tapas Acupressure Technique), *tftrx.com*, and *emofree.com* (psychological acupressure)

umm.edu/altmed/index.htm (University of Maryland Complementary and Alternative Medicine)

watoxics.org/homes-and-gardens/factsheets/vinyl (Washington Toxics Coalition overview)

watoxics.org/homes-and-gardens/resources-treated-wood (treated wood)

watoxics.org/issues/pbde/pbde-resources (safe furniture choices)

Index

About the Author

Sondra Kornblatt is a health and science writer with special interest in wellness, spirituality, and parenting. She originated the Restful Insomnia program, which helps people rest when they can't sleep (*www.RestfulInsomnia.com*). She and her family live in the Pacific Northwest.